THE
StreetSmart Negotiator

THE
StreetSmart Negotiator

How to Outwit, Outmaneuver, and Outlast Your Opponents

Harry Mills

AMACOM
American Management Association
New York • Atlanta • Brussels • Chicago • Mexico City • San Francisco
Shanghai • Tokyo • Toronto • Washington, D.C.

Special discounts on bulk quantities of AMACOM books are available to corporations, professional associations, and other organizations. For details, contact Special Sales Department, AMACOM, a division of American Management Association, 1601 Broadway, New York, NY 10019.
Tel: 212-903-8316 Fax: 212-903-8083

This publication is designed to provide accurate and authorative information in regard to the subject matter covered. It is sold with the understanding that the publisher is not engaged in rendering legal, accounting, or other professional service. If legal advice or other expert assistance is required, the services of a competent professional person should be sought.

Library of Congress Cataloging-in-Publication Data

Mills, Harry.
    The streetsmart negotiator : how to outfox, outmaneuver, and outlast your opponents / Harry Mills.
      p. cm.
  Includes bibliographical references and index.
  ISBN 0-8144-7198-6 (alk. paper)
  1. Negotiation in business. I. Title.

HD58.6.M55 2005
658.4'052—dc22

2005002637

© 2005 Harry Mills All rights reserved.
Printed in the United States of America.

This publication may not be reproduced,
stored in retrieval system,
or transmitted in whole or in part,
in any form or by any means, electronic,
mechanical, photocopying, recording, or otherwise,
without the prior written permission of AMACOM,
a division of American Management Association,
1601 Broadway, New York, NY 10019.

Printing number

10 9 8 7 6 5 4 3 2 1

CONTENTS

Acknowledgments ix
Introduction xi

One: The Seven Steps to Agreement — 3
The Seven Step RESPECT Formula — 4
What is Negotiation — 6
The Bargaining Range — 8

Two: Step 1—Ready Yourself — 11
Use Your BATNA to Create Leverage — 12
Identify Interests — 14
List, Rank, and Value the Issues — 16
Plan Your Agenda — 18
Determine Your Authority — 20
Plan Your First Offer — 22
Pick Your Team — 24
Devise Your Time Plan — 26
Analyze the Other Party — 28
Plan Your Strategy — 30
Assess Your Appetite for Risk — 32
Manage Your Risks — 34
Strive for Fairness — 36
Beware of Deception — 38
Uncover Deceit — 40
Guard Your Reputation — 42

Three: Step 2—Explore Needs — 45
Establish Your Credibility — 46
Communicate Your Position — 48

Create a Positive Nonverbal Climate	50
Influence with Questions	52
Listen to Advantage	54
Use Persuasive Language	56
Words That Sell	58
Use Silence for Advantage	60
Translate the Meta-Talk	62

Four: Step 3—Signal For Movement — 65

How to Signal	66

Five: Step 4—Probe With Proposals — 69

Use Proposals to Generate Movement	70
Package Your Proposals	72

Six: Step 5—Exchange Concessions — 75

Trade for Advantage	76
Open First?	78
Open High?	80
Beware the Gender Trap	82
Slicing the Pie	84
Enlarging the Pie	86
Build Momentum	88

Seven: Step 6—Close the Deal — 91

Manage the Tension	92
When to Close	94
The Summary Close	96
Two More Proven Closes	98
Consider Contingent Contracts	100

Eight: Step 7—Tie Up The Loose Ends — 103

Verify What Has Been Agreed	104
Review Your Performance	106

Nine: Winning Tactics — **109**

   Choose Your Tactics — 110
   Nibble — 112
   Add-On — 114
   Lack of Authority — 116
   Take It or Leave It — 118
   Escalation — 120
   The Budget Limitation — 122
   Good Guy, Bad Guy — 124
   Outrageous Initial Demand — 126
   Chicken — 128
   Reverse Auction — 130

Ten: Persuasion Traps — **133**

   Smart Negotiator, Dumb Deal — 134
   Trap 1: Over-Confidence, Ego, Hubris — 136
   Trap 2: Loss Aversion — 138
   Trap 3: Plunging In — 140
   Trap 4: Anchoring — 142
   Trap 5: Myopia — 144
   Trap 6: Frame Blindness — 146
   Trap 7: Focusing on Vivid Events — 148
   Trap 8: Number Blindness — 150
   Trap 9: Irrational Commitment — 152
   Trap 10: Win-Lose Mindset — 154
   Trap 11: The Lemming Effect — 156
   Trap 12: The Winner's Curse — 158

Eleven: Electronic Bargaining — **161**

   Bargaining on the Telephone — 162
   Negotiating by E-Mail — 164

Twelve: Plan for Success — **167**

   How to Plan a Negotiation — 168
   The Mills One-Page Planner — 169

Appendixes — 171

Appendix A. Assess Your Bargaining Style — 171

Appendix B. Checklist of Body Language Gestures — 176

Appendix C. Checkpoints: Steps 1 to 7—The RESPECT Model — 178

Appendix D. Recommendations for Further Reading — 181

Notes — 185

Index — 189

About the Author — 195

*To Matthew and Ella Steele,
living proof that kids are born negotiators.*

ACKNOWLEDGMENTS

So many people have contributed to my learning on negotiation over the years I now find it a great struggle to say exactly where a particular idea originated. I do, however, wish to thank David Lax, Roger Fisher, and the staff at the Harvard Negotiation Project, who were so generous with their time way back in 1989 and encouraged me to start writing on negotiating.

I owe a tremendous debt to my many clients and seminar participants who have helped to test and refine the materials.

I want to especially thank all those who agreed to review the manuscript in its various drafts.

Finally, there is my wife, Mary Anne. She has now put up with me for twenty-four books, and that fact alone demands special acknowledgment. Without her unwaivering love and support these books would never have been possible.

INTRODUCTION

Before I started writing this book I drew up a list of the features I believed a negotiation field guide should contain.

First and foremost a negotiation field guide has to be *practical.* A handbook must not only be interesting, it must be useful. The tips, techniques and strategies should have been field tested and the examples drawn from real life.

A handbook must be *user-friendly.* Information must be readable and easily accessed. The test of a good handbook is how fast you can access the information you're searching for. A user friendly handbook has a comprehensive list of contents, a good index, lots of subheadings, checklists of key points, and is attractively designed.

However, while effective handbooks are simple to follow, they are never simplistic. Negotiation is a complex subject which takes time to master. Authors who reduce the subject to four or five key commandments or principles do their readers a disservice.

A negotiation handbook whose goal is to help readers become better negotiators must focus on the skills it takes to become a top negotiator. Anyone who has run skill-based negotiation seminars knows it is not enough to tell participants to ask questions and actively listen. You also have to show them how to question and listen. An effective negotiation handbook must do the same.

The central thrust in any negotiation handbook should be on how to facilitate win-win negotiations. This is not simply a matter of ethical preference, it is good business. The vast majority of negotiations most people find themselves in are situations where it is in their self-interest to create a solution that is good for both sides. Negotiations based on mutual satisfaction work better, are essential for long-term relationships, and lead to repeat business.

Nevertheless, life in the real world means you also have to negotiate with ruthless or unethical operators. A handbook that ignores this fact and doesn't show you how to cope or urges you to rely on trust and goodwill is naïve and dangerous.

The book is organized around the seven identifiable steps that make up the negotiation process. Apart from the logic of starting at the beginning with the preparation step and ending up with how to tie up the loose ends, the steps are a useful memory and training aid. Different skills and abilities are used in each step. And once you can identify what step you are in you can plan your course of action. Inexperienced negotiators often skip the early steps, rush into trading concessions, lose control, and end up with a bad deal.

Negotiators who follow the seven steps and who can identify what they need to do, keep control. Control breeds confidence and results in even better deals.

I have always been fascinated why so many smart negotiators negotiate what in retrospect are "dumb deals." *The StreetSmart Negotiator* exposes those traps and shows negotiators how to avoid becoming entrapped.

THE
StreetSmart
Negotiator

R-E-S-P-E-C-T

The seven steps to agreement

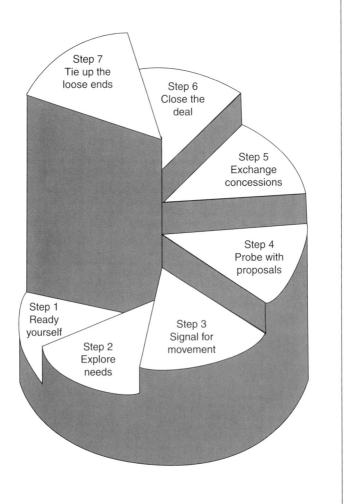

Chapter One

THE SEVEN STEPS TO AGREEMENT

Negotiation is the art of letting them have your way.
      Daniele Vare
      italian diplomat

4

The Seven Step RESPECT Formula

Negotiation is a seven step process. The seven steps form the acronym RESPECT.

The Seven Steps

Step One: **R**eady yourself. You set and prioritize your objectives and plan your strategy and techniques.

Step Two: **E**xplore each other's needs. You clarify your and the other side's needs and communicate your opening position.

Step Three: **S**ignal for movement. You signal that you are prepared to move and respond to signals from the other side.

Step Four: **P**robe with proposals. To advance the negotiation you make tentative proposals and repackage rejected proposals.

Step Five: **E**xchange concessions. Here you trade concessions by giving the other party some of their demands in exchange for receiving part of what you want.

Step Six: **C**lose the deal. Create urgency by making a credible and acceptable close.

Step Seven: **T**ie-up the loose ends. Having agreed you have a deal you must confirm exactly what has been agreed.

> Anyone who doesn't think there are two sides to an argument is probably in one!
>
> SAM HORN
> COMMUNICATIONS EXPERT
> AUTHOR, *TONGUE FU!*

Smart Tips & Tactics

■ **Manage the process, shape the result.** Lose control of the process and you'll end up with a bad deal.

■ **Spend most of your time planning and exploring needs.** Spend 60 percent to 70 percent of your time doing your homework and questioning for needs.

■ **Avoid the temptation to skip steps.** Never start trading concessions until you have checked out all your assumptions.

■ **Take your time.** Rushed deals often turn sour.

■ **Think co-opetition when you negotiate.** Negotiation involves competition where you compete for a share of the pie. Negotiation involves cooperation where you collaborate and share interests.

Managing the Process:

Whoever controls the process powerfully influences the substance and outcomes of negotiations. This is especially true in complex situations that allow one to take advantage of the fog of negotiation.

MICHAEL WATKINS
ASSOCIATE PROFESSOR OF BUSINESS ADMINISTRATION AT HARVARD BUSINESS SCHOOL, WHERE HE TEACHES NEGOTIATION AND CORPORATE DIPLOMACY[1]

What is Negotiation?

Getting What We Want
We all negotiate because negotiation is simply a very effective way of getting what we want. We negotiate to settle our differences and we negotiate out of self-interest to satisfy our needs.

In negotiation both sides have common interests and conflicting interests. Unless both are present, a negotiation is pointless.

When Do We Negotiate?
We only negotiate when the alternatives to negotiation—that is, no agreement—are worse. Unions strike rather than negotiate because they believe a strike will result in greater gains than talks. Employers lock out their workers, nations fight each other, and litigants battle each other in court for similar reasons.

Give and Take
We often confuse negotiation with other forms of conflict resolution. You know you are in negotiation if you have the authority and ability to vary the terms—to give as well as take. Negotiations, in essence, involve trading concessions.

> When a person with money meets a person with experience, the person with the experience winds up with the money and the person with the money ends up with the experience.
>
> HARVEY MACKAY
> BUSINESSMAN
> AND AUTHOR

Smart Tips & Tactics

■ **Use a skilled negotiator to review all your major negotiations.** Lack of immediate feedback is the prime reason why we continue to repeat the same fundamental errors.

■ **Don't settle for mediocrity.** Most negotiators settle for less than the other side is prepared to give.

■ **Experiment with new persuasion and negotiation techniques.** You'll be amazed how many deals can be turned from win-lose to win-win.

■ **Practice, practice, practice.** Take every opportunity, small and large, to test and sharpen your negotiation and persuasion skills.

StreetTalk

Leaving money on the table occurs when negotiators fail to recognize and exploit win-win potential. Settling for too little occurs when negotiators make too-large concessions. Walking away from the table occurs when negotiators reject terms offered by the other party that are demonstrably better than any other option. Settling for terms that are worse than your alternative occurs when negotiators feel obliged to reach agreement even when the settlement terms are not as good as their other alternatives.

LEIGH THOMPSON
PROFESSOR OF MANAGEMENT
KELLOGG GRADUATE SCHOOL
AUTHOR, *THE MIND AND HEART OF THE NEGOTIATOR*[2]

8

The Bargaining Range

Zone of Possible Agreement
As both sides move through the negotiation process and move closer towards each other and agreement, they move into The Bargaining Range or Zone of Possible Agreement (ZOPA).

This is best shown in a diagram. Consider an industrialist and property owner negotiating over the price of a warehouse. The owner of the building has asked for $7,000,000 and will not drop below $4,000,000 (his reserve price). He does not know it but the industrialist could go up to $5,000,000 (her reserve price).

> In baiting a mouse trap with cheese, always leave room for the mouse.
>
> Saki
> Scottish writer

Reservation Prices
The bargaining range runs from the seller's reserve price to the buyer's reserve price. The settlement will be reached somewhere in this *Zone of Possible Agreement.*

Zone of Possible Agreement

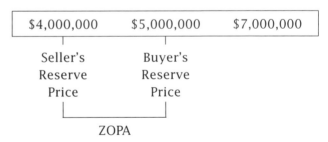

Smart Tips & Tactics

■ **Negotiations are built on movement.** Unless the parties are prepared to move into the zone of possible agreement, the negotiation will deadlock.

■ **Use the midpoint between the two opening offers to predict what the parties will finally agree to.** This is provided the midpoint is within the zone of possible agreement.

■ **Most negotiators have a range of possible settlement points.** These range from their most optimistic to their most pessimistic.

■ **In most negotiations, neither side really knows what the other side's reservation price is.** To reveal your resistance price in a negotiation is usually self-defeating.

■ **Watch out for negative bargaining zones.** Don't waste your time trying to bargain where there is no possible zone of agreement.

Once two offers are on the table . . . the best prediction of the final contract is the midpoint . . . provided that the midpoint falls within the zone of possible agreement.

HOWARD RAIFFA
WITH JOHN RICHARDSON AND
DAVID METCALFE
NEGOTIATION ANALYSIS[3]

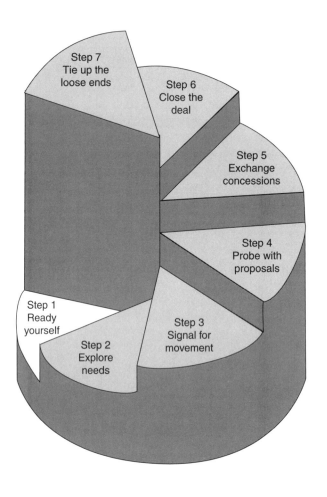

Chapter Two

STEP 1 READY YOURSELF

If I had nine hours to cut down a tree, I would spend six hours sharpening my axe!

>   ABRAHAM LINCOLN
>   16TH PRESIDENT OF THE UNITED STATES

Features
In Step One You: **Ready** yourself. Here you:

- Set and prioritize your objectives.
- Identify your interests.
- Identify, rank, and value your issues.
- Determine what concessions you can give and what concessions you need in return.
- Define your BATNA.
- Gather as much information as you can.
- Plan your strategy and supporting tactics.

12

Use Your BATNA to Create Leverage

What Is BATNA?
Before you even start negotiating, work out your BATNA. A BATNA is your *Best Alternative To a Negotiated Agreement.* When you work out your best alternative in a negotiation you are calculating your walk-away position.

Any agreement you reach must satisfy your interests *better* than you could be exercising your BATNA.

Harvard professors Roger Fisher and William Ury coined the acronym BATNA to persuade negotiators to move away from using unrealistic, unflexible bottom lines.

Your BATNA Is Your Power Base
Armed with a strong BATNA you can negotiate with confidence and power. On the other hand, if your BATNA is worse than you hoped, you should temper your demand.

How to Work Out Your BATNA
A BATNA involves three stages: First, list everything you could do if you do not reach agreement. Second, explore your best options and try to improve on them. Finally, choose the best option. This is your BATNA.

> Power is wonderful, and absolute power is absolutely wonderful.
>
> H. ROSS PEROT
> BUSINESSMAN, DEALMAKER AND PRESIDENTIAL CANDIDATE

Smart Tips & Tactics

■ **Always consider the other party's BATNA.** Remember, the better their BATNA, the stronger their bargaining position.

■ **If the other party's offers are better than your BATNA, take them.** If the offers are worse, bargain to improve them.

■ **Don't confront the other side with your BATNA too early.** Try to sell the merits and fairness of your case first.

■ **If a negotiation is going badly, don't hesitate to reveal your BATNA.** It can increase your leverage.

■ **Don't reveal your BATNA if it is worse than the other side already imagines.** You will only weaken your case.

> *If you're strong, make sure your counterpart knows it. If you're weak, work hard to keep him from realizing it.*
>
> *If your counterpart believes he's stronger than he actually is, educate him to the real facts. If he thinks he's weaker than he actually is, don't say a word!*
>
> JAMES C. FREUND
> PROMINENT TAKEOVER SPECIALIST AND NEGOTIATOR[1]

14

Identify Interests

Dig Behind Positions

The purpose of negotiating is to satisfy your interests or underlying needs.

Positions are the stands we take on *what* we want, interests are the *underlying* needs that motivate us to ask. Too often in negotiations we forget we have to reconcile our interests. Foolishly, we concentrate on our positions.

Reconcile Interests

Two sisters, Amy and Alicia, quarrel over the last orange in the fruit bowl. Enter Mother: "Enough of this arguing," she says and she grabs a knife and cuts the orange in two. The 50-50 split seems as fair as you can imagine. Yet when Mother later checks on the girls, she finds Amy has squeezed the juice out of her half orange for a drink, while Alicia has used the peel of her half orange in a cake she is baking.

If both sides had taken the time to use questions to dig behind their stated positions, Amy could have had all the juice; Alicia, all the peel.

> Whenever you're sitting across from some important person, always picture him sitting there in a suit of long red underwear. That's the way I've always operated in business.
>
> JOSEPH P. KENNEDY
> BUSINESSMAN AND DIPLOMAT

Smart Tips & Tactics

- **To identify your interests, examine each position and ask:**
  - Why am I taking this stand?
  - What purpose does this position serve?
  - Why is this important to me?
  - What will achieving this help me do?
  - What will happen if I don't achieve this?

- **To identify the other side's interests:**
  - List each of the points you want them to agree to.
  - Ask what might stop them agreeing to your requests? The answers will very likely include their interests.

- **Don't forget to dig for long-term interests.** These are often the key to agreement.

> Don't assume that you know what people want, or that they know what you want—just because you know one another well. Get the facts or the facts will get you.
>
> KARE ANDERSON
> AUTHOR AND SPEAKER
> ON PERSUASION AND NEGOTIATION[2]

16

List, Rank, and Value the Issues

List the Issues
Once you have identified your interests, start drawing up an issue list. To turn your interests into tradable issues ask yourself, "If the other side agrees with me what exactly do I want to do?"

Rank the Issues
Rank your issues into three groups:
High priority. Your *must* gets. These are your essentials. If you don't achieve these, use your BATNA and walk away from the negotiation table.
Medium priority. Your *should* gets. You expect to achieve these. You will be very disappointed if you don't achieve most of them.
Low priority. Your *could* gets. You would like to achieve these. But these are your tradables.

Value Every Issue
Professional negotiators know what every issue on the table is worth. Virtually any item in a business negotiation can be reduced to an objective monetary value.

Price each issue within a specific range—stretching from your minimum to your maximum settlement point.

> Pick battles big enough to matter, small enough to win.
> JONATHAN KOZOL
> AUTHOR

Smart Tips & Tactics

■ **List as many issues as you can.** The more issues or variables there are, the more tradables.

■ **Value what each issue is worth to you.** Then ask, "What is each one worth to the other party?"

■ **After listing your objectives do the same for the other party.** Ask:
- What do they really want?
- How far can they go on each issue?
- What are their priorities?

■ **Finally, compare their priorities to yours.** Each difference offers a potential trading opportunity. You are now ready to draw up a list of possible trades.

■ **Think win-win.** The goal is to trade what is cheap for you for what is valuable to the other side.

In all negotiations, there are two things being bargained for: The specific issues and demands, which are stated openly. The real needs of the other side, which are rarely verbalized.

HERB COHEN
AUTHOR, SPEAKER
DESCRIBED BY *PLAYBOY* MAGAZINE
AS THE "WORLDS BEST NEGOTIATOR"

18

Plan Your Agenda

List and Order the Issues
Use an agenda to control the flow and direction of your negotiation.

Use your agenda to:
- List the issues you want discussed.
- Establish the order in which you want to deal with them.
- Define how you want to deal with the issues.
- Set approximate time limits for agenda items.
- Set procedure rules.

With their agenda, ask:
- Does the agenda cover everything I want discussed?
- Are there any issues I want to avoid?
- Are there any issues I consider non-negotiable?
- What does the agenda tell me about their strategy and priorities?

Be prepared to negotiate the agenda. In hostile negotiations it can take real skill to get the other side to even consider an agenda.

> Plans are nothing; planning is everything.
>
> DWIGHT D. EISENHOWER
> 34TH PRESIDENT OF THE UNITED STATES

Smart Tips & Tactics

■ **If possible, use your agenda.** It gives you control of the process.

■ **Don't accept an agenda that disadvantages you.** Once you lose control of a negotiation it's difficult to regain it.

■ **Start with the minor issues first** when you have many points to negotiate.

■ **If it makes sense, block issues into logical chunks.** This is often the easier way to proceed.

■ **Note the issues that you want to avoid.** Don't undermine your chances by raising issues in which you are weak.

■ **Allocate plenty of time to discuss what is important to you.** It takes time to persuade people, especially on contentious issues.

Street Talk

Always try to negotiate the agenda before talks begin. The negotiator who controls the agenda controls what will be said and perhaps more important, what will not be said.

DR. CHESTER L. KARASS
VETERAN NEGOTIATOR,
AUTHOR, AND FOUNDER OF THE
CENTER FOR EFFECTIVE NEGOTIATING[3]

Determine Your Authority

Know Your Limit
If you negotiate on behalf of somebody else, you will need to meet with them to set the limits of your authority to negotiate each issue. This is essential. If you ever make a deal and your principal reneges, your credibility soon evaporates.

> The longer the title, the less important the job.
>
> GEORGE MCGOVERN
> U.S. SENATOR
> DEMOCRATIC PARTY
> NOMINEE FOR PRESIDENT

To Determine Their Authority, Ask:
How do you go about making decisions such as this?
Who gets involved in making these decisions?
How much time do decisions such as these usually take?
Does the company have a purchasing policy and may I see a copy?

Limits Increase Confidence
Negotiators who are unsure of their authority are in a weak position. If you know your limit, you are more commanding and assertive. The confidence that comes from knowing you will be backed up, strengthens your position.

Smart Tips & Tactics

- **Never admit during a negotiation to having total authority.** It takes away your flexibility and limits your options.

- **If your opponent puts you on the spot and asks,** "Can you finalize the deal?" reply, "Yes, if it is within the limits set by my principal."

- **Beware of the "no authority here" tactic.** Always ask the other negotiator if they have full authority to settle. Don't always believe the answer. Negotiators don't like admitting to being the "monkey" and not the "organ grinder."

Negotiating with people without authority to settle is like being at an auction, except you are often only bidding against yourself. The other party forces you to change your offer because it is not yet good enough for acceptance by the higher authority.

GAVIN KENNEDY
BEST-SELLING AUTHOR OF NINE BOOKS ON NEGOTIATION,
SCOTTISH BUSINESS SCHOOL PROFESSOR AND FREELANCE NEGOTIATING SKILLS CONSULTANT[4]

Plan Your First Offer

Plan Carefully
Before you start bargaining, calculate your initial offer. More than any other single factor, your first offer will shape the outcome of the final deal. And remember you'll never get more than you ask for.

If your offer is too high, it may be rejected out of hand. If your offer is too low, it may be taken as a sign of weakness.

Aim High
Research shows that negotiators who make more extreme opening offers get more than their counterparts who make low or modest offers. However, extreme offers are also more likely to be summarily rejected.

Multiply Your Variables
When you aim high, create flexibility by multiplying the issues under discussion. Single issue negotiations often deadlock. Not only does starting high as a strategy give you more room to make concessions but also the other party seems to gauge their success by the size of the concessions they extract.

> We think too small. Like the frog at the bottom of the well. He thinks the sky is only as big as the top of the well. If he surfaced, he would have an entirely different view.
>
> Mao Ze-dong
> Chinese Communist Leader

Smart Tips & Tactics

■ **Aim high.** But make sure your offer is realistic and credible. If you can't justify your initial offer with logic and reason, don't use it.

■ **Practice defending your initial offer.** Find someone to role-play your opponent.

■ **Don't communicate uncertainty when talking price.** Phrases such as "about" or "in the range of" communicate tentativeness.

■ **Avoid excessive detail, especially on price breakdowns.** Too much detail can destroy your flexibility and allows you to be more easily played off against the competition.

■ **Use confident, assertive language.** Speak as though you expect your offer to be accepted.

StreetTalk

All other things being equal, the first offer has more influence on the final deal than any other factor. People who make generous first offers get worse deals than people who make ungenerous ones.

ALAN N. SCHOONMAKER
NEGOTIATION RESEARCHER,
CONSULTANT AND AUTHOR[5]

24

Pick Your Team

> When building a team, I always search first for people who love to win. If I can't find any of those, I look for people who hate to lose.
>
> H. Ross Perot
> BUSINESSMAN,
> DEALMAKER AND
> PRESIDENTIAL
> CANDIDATE

Teams Achieve More
Some negotiators prefer acting alone. They like the extra control it gives.

A well-organized, well-led team, however, is difficult to beat. Even the simplest negotiation is complex. It is rare to find a negotiator who can talk, listen, watch, think and plan at the same time.

When it comes to analysing the mass of facts and technical data that often passes across the negotiation table, two or more heads usually cope better than one.

A Well-Managed Team:
- Allows multiple interests to be represented.
- Builds commitment to the final agreement.
- Raises the confidence and assertiveness of all its members.
- Is a formidable opponent.

A Poorly Managed Team:
- Will split into factions.
- Will give away critical information to the other side.
- Lacks direction.

Don't form teams simply to match the other team's numbers. A small tightly organized team will out-negotiate most large teams.

Smart Tips & Tactics

- **Allocate specific functions to different team members.** They need to take on four key tasks.
  - **Appoint a team leader.** Task: to handle all the face-to-face bargaining. The leader orchestrates the play, does most of the talking, raises new issues, makes proposals and trades concessions.
  - **Appoint a reviewer.** Task: to summarize the progress to date and clarify points with questions.
  - **Appoint an observer.** Task: to watch and monitor the verbal and non-verbal messages.
  - **Appoint an analyst.** Task: to record and analyze all the numbers and other data. The pattern of offers and concessions invariably provides insights into the other side's objectives and priorities.

StreetTalk

Forming teams on the basis of matching the other team's numbers is not very sensible. A well-briefed team need not be the same size as the other side's. There's 'no safety in numbers,' only expense.

GAVIN KENNEDY
AUTHOR OF NINE BOOKS ON NEGOTIATION, SCOTTISH BUSINESS SCHOOL PROFESSOR AND FREELANCE NEGOTIATING SKILLS CONSULTANT[6]

Devise Your Time Plan

Watch for Time Pressure
Deadlines cause negotiators to soften their demands. When negotiators are under time pressure, they lower their aspirations, bluff less frequently and make more concessions. Knowing your opponent's deadline will give you an edge, so don't reveal your deadlines to the other side unless you have to.

Manage Your Time Frame
To counter deadline pressure, prepare a time plan. Anticipate what you will do if the negotiation drags. Prepare for evasive action.

In a Deadline Trap:
- Ask yourself, is there any way I can extend my own deadline?
- Ask yourself, what can I do to alter the deadline pressures being used by the other party?

Be Prepared to Walk Away
Sometimes it is better to walk away from a deal. Deals rarely get worse when you walk away from the table. Usually when you return you find you can negotiate even better terms.

> Next week there can't be any crisis. My schedule is already full.
>
> HENRY A. KISSINGER
> FORMER U.S.
> SECRETARY OF STATE

Smart Tips & Tactics

■ **To counter deadline pressure, be patient.** Act as though there is plenty of time available.

■ **Use deadlines to create momentum.** If a deadline doesn't exist, create one.

■ **Creative incentives for a quick agreement,** if you suffer from a deadline disadvantage.

■ **Watch the time trap.** The more time you invest in a negotiation, the more committed you become to a deal.

■ **Guard against time entrapment.** Fix a date for the completion of the negotiations beyond which you will not go.

> *The "other side," cool and serene as they may appear, always have a deadline. Most often the tranquillity they display outwardly masks a great deal of stress and pressure.*
>
> HERB COHEN
> AUTHOR, SPEAKER AND PRACTITIONER
> DESCRIBED BY *PLAYBOY* magazine AS THE
> WORLD'S BEST NEGOTIATOR

Analyze the Other Party

Do Your Homework
Knowing and understanding the other side is central to success.

Your Analysis Should Include
- The other party's interests.
- The other party's goals and priorities.
- The strengths and weaknesses of their negotiators.
- The other party's constituency. How involved will they be?
- The other party's reputation.
- The other party's style. Is it competitive or co-operative?
- The other party's BATNA. This determines their power base.
- The other party's authority level.
- The other party's likely strategy and techniques.
- The other party's deadline.
- The other party's budget in a financial deal.

Bluffs
Some opponents love to bluff. However bluffing works only against opponents who are unprepared. Gain a reputation for doing your homework, and the bluffing you face will drop markedly.

> Once the toothpaste is out of the tube, it's hard to get it back in.
>
> H.R. HALDEMAN
> PRESIDENT NIXON'S WHITE HOUSE CHIEF OF STAFF JAILED FOR HIS ROLE IN WATERGATE SCANDAL

Smart Tips & Tactics

- **To identify the other side's interests:**
  - List each of the points you want them to agree to.
  - Ask what might stop them agreeing to your requests. These answers will very likely include their interests.
  - Interview others who have negotiated with them in the past. Past negotiating behavior is the best clue to future behavior.

- **To uncover the other party's objectives, ask them.** Meetings that precede the actual negotiations are usually goldmines of information.

- **Compare their BATNA,** reputation, style, authority and objectives to yours. This helps you determine their strategy.

- **Calculate their deadline.** The greater the urgency the more they will concede.

Disastrous Deal: *In 1989 Ford purchased the luxury car maker Jaguar for $2.5 billion. Since then Jaguar has continued to run up multimillion-dollar losses. In 2004, a car insurance analyst calculated that the losses amounted to over $6,000 for every car sold.*

Plan Your Strategy

Your Strategy Is Your Game Plan

To get what you want from others, the best approach is usually to help the other party get what *they* want.

However, we also have to negotiate with hardliners who don't care about our needs. They are win-lose negotiators—they win, you lose. You may also adopt a win-lose strategy if you feel there is nothing to gain from mutual collaboration.

> Expect the worst and your surprises will always be pleasant ones.
>
> LOUISE E. BOON
> EDUCATOR AND
> BUSINESS WRITER

Therefore, you should always be able to adapt your strategy to fit the situation.

The Four Strategy Choices

Their Needs		
	Lose-Win	Win-Win
	Lose-Lose	Win-Lose
	Your Needs	

Smart Tips & Tactics

Ask these questions when determining your strategy:

▪ **Is there going to be a continuing relationship?** In a one-off deal the incentives to be open and cooperative are less.

▪ **What are the relative strengths of the parties?** The difference in the balance of power can strongly influence the approach.

▪ **How much truth exists?** A win-win strategy requires trust and openness. This usually takes time.

▪ **What do we know about the personality and style of the other side?** Some negotiators are ruthlessly competitive.

▪ **How much time is available?** The side with a time advantage can adopt a tougher approach.

> *All men can see those tactics whereby I conquer, but what none can see is the strategy out of which victory is evolved.*
>
> SUN-TZU
> FOURTH CENTURY B.C. CHINESE MILITARY STRATEGIST

Assess Your Appetite for Risk

Your appetite for risk will have a big impact on how and what you negotiate.

Risk Taker?
Are you a risk taker? Do you enjoy the thrill that comes from negotiating high-risk, high-reward deals? Negotiating a complex deal can be like navigating your way across a minefield, so you need to be able to anticipate where it is safe or potentially hazardous to tread.

Risk Averse?
Are you risk averse? Do you prefer to minimize your risks and walk away from deals where there are large potential downside losses—even where the upside rewards are great?

Risk Neutral?
Or would you describe yourself as risk neutral? Do you approach risk like an investment analyst, carefully calculating the risks and rewards for each deal?

> Progress always involves risks. You can't steal second base while keeping your foot on first.
>
> FREDERICK WILCOX
> WRITER

Smart Tips & Tactics

■ **Make risk assessment a key part of your deal preparation.** Before every deal assess the level of risk you are willing to assume.

■ **If you're inherently cautious don't try to turn yourself into a high-wheeling risk taker.** When personality and deal risk move out of alignment, bad decisions usually follow.

■ **Remember high reward does not always mean high risks.** Careful risk management can achieve high returns.

■ **Learn to love boredom.** High-risk deals have a habit of turning to custard and causing long-term heartache.

■ **Use the "will I sleep at night" test.** Before signing any deal ask, if this deal turns sour will I sleep at night? If your answer is no, do not proceed.

StreetTalk

Avoiding Risk: *Corbin Robertson owns the largest private coal reserves in the USA—21 billion tons. In 1969, Robertson lost money when he tried to mine a deposit that was riddled with Civil War tunnels. Ever since, Robertson has let experienced operators carry the risk and costs of mining while he collects a predictable—and insulated—royalty and annual fee for every ton extracted. "If a mining operation goes bust, Robertson keeps the equipment and leases the mine to somebody else."*

FORBES GLOBAL[7]

34

Manage Your Risks

Complacency is a negotiator's worst enemy. Every deal has its risks and each one needs to be actively managed.

How to Approach Risk Management
There are lots of ways to approach risk management. Most, however, are far too complicated to be of much practical use to negotiators.

The O'Connell Formula
Project management expert Fergus O'Connell has developed a simple but highly practical approach to risk management, which I've found works well in most negotiations. His approach to risk management is incorporated into the form on the opposite page.

To manage deal risks:
- Estimate the likelihood of each of these risk occurring.
- Assess the impact of each of the risks.
- Calculate the exposure to each risk.
- Identify the actions you need to reduce your risks.

In one of his famous saloon scenes, the wily actor and comedian W.C. Fields is intently studying his poker hand. An observer asks, "Mr. Fields, is this a game of chance?" Fields pauses, then replies, "Not the way I play it!"

Risk Management Form

Risks	Likelihood	Impact	Exposure	Actions
	1 = low	1 = low	Multiply	
	2 = medium	2 = medium	Likelihood ×	
	3 = high	3 = high	Impact	

Strive for Fairness

> He's fair. He treats us all the same—like dogs.
>
> HENRY JORDAN
> AMERICAN FOOTBALL PLAYER
> (REFERRING TO GREEN BAY PACKERS' COACH VINCE LOMBARDI)

A Bitter Divorce

In 1997 Gary Wendt, the chief executive of GE Capital, divorced his fifty-four-year-old wife of thirty-two years, Lorna Wendt. Gary's net worth was about $100 million. Lorna wanted a 50-50 split. In court, Gary argued that since it was his talents that accumulated virtually all of the wealth he was entitled to the bulk of the assets. The judge awarded Lorna $20 million. Divorce law in Connecticut calls for equitable not equal distribution of assets.

Principles of Fairness

Our notions of fairness are guided by three, often conflicting, principles:

1. The principle of **equality** says that regardless of contribution, everyone is entitled to an equal share.

2. The principle of ***equity*** prescribes that rewards should be based on each person's contribution.

3. The principle of **need** prescribes that benefits should be based on need.

Smart Tips & Tactics

■ **When slicing up the cake, always ask to whom will the recipient(s) compare themselves.** People often care more about how their slice compares to others than they do about the absolute size of the pie.

■ **Make sure the process is seen to be fair and equitable.** Commitment to a deal increases when the process is viewed as just and transparent.

■ **Aim for simplicity, clarity and justifiability.** Perceptions of fairness increase when agreements are simple to follow, deliver clear outcomes and can be easily explained.

■ **Remember, our egos clash with our notions of fairness.** People pay themselves far more than they are willing to pay others for the same job.

Street Talk

An Aesop Fable on Fairness: *Several animals find a treasure and must decide how to divide it fairly. The lion speaks up and says, "First, we must carefully divide the treasure into four parts. The first part goes to me, since I am king of the beasts. The second part is mine, owing to my strength. The third part is mine because of my courage. As to the fourth part, anyone who cares to dispute it with me can do so, at his own risk."*

Beware of Deception

Lying is Widespread
Lying in negotiation is endemic. One recent study found 28 percent of negotiators lied about a common interest during negotiations.
Another study revealed that one hundred percent of negotiators either failed to reveal a problem or actively lied about it during negotiations if they were not directly asked about the issue.

> When a man tells me he's going to put all his cards on the table, I always look up his sleeve.
>
> Lord Hore-Belisha
> British Secretary for War 1937–1940

Omission or Commission
Lies of omission (not revealing information) are more common than lies of commission (actively misrepresenting information). Wharton researcher Maurice Schweitzer found negotiators lie about:

- **Reservation prices.** Virtually everyone lies when it comes to stating their bottomline or reservation price.
- **Interests.** Negotiators often mislead their counterparts over their real interests. For example, a negotiator may portray a common interest as a conflicting interest in order to win a concession.
- **Intentions.** Negotiators often try to bluff the other side by misrepresenting their intentions.
- **Material facts.** Intentional false statements about material facts can constitute fraud.

Smart Tips & Tactics

■ **Guard against deception.** The best way to curtail deception is to reduce the odds of it ever occurring in the first place.

■ **Ask direct questions.** Research shows negotiators are much less likely to lie when faced with a direct question.

■ **Turn all your information gaps and assumptions into questions.** Then test for consistency by asking multiple variations of the same question.

■ **Research the other party's reputation.** You need to protect yourself against negotiators who are prepared to lie and manipulate to gain an advantage.

■ **Keep a written record of all verbal claims and assurances.** Negotiators are less likely to lie when written records are kept.

■ **Verify material information wherever possible.** Negotiators are much more honest when they know you are prepared to check out any claims or representations.

■ **Ask for written representations and warranties.** Don't just take their word at face value. Ask them to write it down and warrant that it is true in a legally binding agreement.

Street Talk

He that has eyes to see and ears to hear may convince himself that no mortal can keep a secret. If his lips are silent, he chatters with his fingertips; betrayal oozes out of him at every pore.

SIGMUND FREUD
AUSTRIAN DOCTOR WHO REVOLUTIONALIZED THE PRACTICE OF PSYCHIATRY

Uncover Deceit

> You can observe a lot just by watching.
>
> YOGI BERRA
> AMERICAN BASEBALL PLAYER AND MANAGER

Humans Are Poor Lie Detectors

The problem is that when it comes to detecting lies, we are not very good.

In a study carried out at the University of California, Dr. Paul Ekman found most of the people we expect to be skilled lie detectors—police detectives, judges and lawyers—are 45 to 60 percent accurate in spotting lies. This is no better than the average citizen.

Training Helps

Training in lie detection, however, can make a big difference. Lie-catching scores usually improve from 50 percent to over 80 percent.

Nonverbal Clues Are the Key

Closely observing nonverbal skills is the key to lie detection. "Everyone knows when we use words, we can say whatever we want, but it takes extraordinary skills to deceive the trained eye with our face, voice and body," says Dr. Ekman.

Common Clues to Deceit

Face
- Avoids eye contact
- Eye pupils dilate and blinking reduces
- Little smiling
- False smiles linger longer and end abruptly
- Smile appears forced
- Eyes seem vacant

Body
- Gestures and words don't match
- Fewer arm and hand movements to illustrate points
- Increased self-touching—nose, chin, mouth

Voice
- Raised voice pitch
- Increased pauses and hesitations
- Slower speech

Words
- Avoids making factual statements
- Uses generalizations instead of specifics
- Words seem forced
- Takes longer to answer questions
- Briefer answers than normal
- More um's and uh's
- Inclined to mumble and speak inexpressively
- Statements sound like questions
- Avoids using pronouns I and We
- Implies rather than gives an answer
- Avoids direct answers
- Uses phrases such as "to be perfectly honest" or "to tell you the truth"
- Claims sound "too good to be true"
- Reasoning sounds implausible
- All the numbers mentioned are rounded and sound the same or are multiples of each other
- Prone to verbal outbursts, which leak information
- Verbal slips of the tongue.

42

Guard Your Reputation

Your Reputation Matters
When you negotiate, your reputation precedes you and has a major impact on the way others negotiate with you.

The Four Reputation Types
Wharton researchers have classified negotiators into four reputation types:
Liar/Manipulator: will do anything to gain an advantage.
Tough but Honest: very tough negotiator, but doesn't lie, makes few concessions.
Nice and Reasonable: will make concessions/be conciliatory.
Cream Puff: will make concessions/be conciliatory regardless of what you do.

Responding in Kind
The researchers found negotiators vary their tactics according to the reputation of their counterparts.
Against *liars,* negotiators commonly use hardball or distributive (win-lose) tactics.
Against *tough* opponents, negotiators use hardball distributive tactics.
Against *nice* counterparts, negotiators adopt integrative or win-win tactics and share lots more information.
Against *cream puffs,* negotiators use hardball, distributive tactics. Cream puffs cave in when faced with aggressive demands.

> Do not be so sweet that people will eat you up, nor so bitter that they will spit you out.
> — PASHTO FOLK SAYING

Smart Tips & Tactics

■ **Cultivate a reputation for being fair and reasonable.** This is the key to building successful long-term relationships.

■ **Cultivate a reputation for toughness,** especially if you work in an environment where dog-eat-dog and highly competitive tactics predominate.

■ **Don't become a victim of your reputation.** Surprise your opponent by occasionally doing the unexpected.

■ **Ask: What is the most effective style to achieve my aims?** Then match your style to the deal.

■ **The most successful negotiators combine toughness with flexibility.** Flexibility shows you're prepared to work hard to achieve a win-win.

Street Talk

I study people, and in every negotiation, I weigh how tough I should appear. I can be a killer and a nice guy. You have to be everything. You have to be strong. You have to be sweet. You have to be ruthless.

DONALD TRUMP
PROPERTY DEVELOPER AND CASINO OWNER

R-E-S-P-E-C-T

The seven steps to agreement

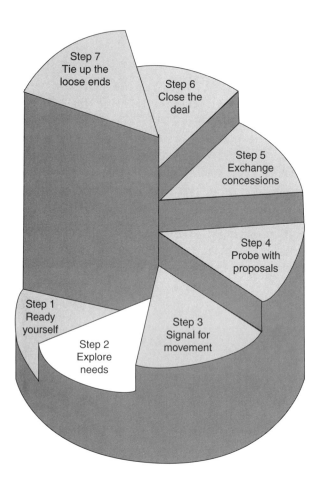

Chapter Three

STEP 2 EXPLORE NEEDS

If I had nine hours to cut down a tree, I would spend six hours sharpening my axe!

    ABRAHAM LINCOLN

Features
In Step Two you: **Explore** each other's needs. You meet face-to-face to:

- Clarify your and the other side's needs.
- Test your assumptions.
- Build rapport to create a win-win climate.
- Communicate your opening position.
- Learn the other side's opening position.

Establish Your Credibility

Once you have completed your preparations, you're ready to meet face to face with the other party. In step two of the negotiation process you explore each other's needs and communicate your opening positions.

The Credibility Formula
When you meet someone for the first time, your first challenge is to establish your credibility. The more credible you are in a negotiation, the more persuasive you are. If the other side doesn't believe you're telling the truth, they will discount everything you say. Think of credibility as a formula: trust + expertise = credibility

Trust Is Based on Reliability
People with dishonest reputations don't get believed—even when they tell the truth. Professional negotiators therefore jealously protect their reputations for honesty.

Expertise Enhances Persuasion
If you're seen as an expert, people listen to your arguments and concede points more often. When people listen to a presentation they constantly ask themselves: Is this person an authority on the subject, and if so how reliable is he or she?

> To be persuasive, we must be believable. To be believable, we must be credible. To be credible, we must be truthful.
>
> EDWARD R. MURROW
> JOURNALIST

Smart Tips & Tactics

■ **Don't oversell your position with exaggerated claims.** Exaggerations weaken the rest of your case.

■ **Never claim more than you think they'll believe.** Your product or service may be the best, but if you can't convince them you're better off moderating your claims.

■ **Point out the disadvantages in your product or service.** It gives credibility to everything else you say.

■ **Build up a portfolio of reputable third-party endorsements and testimonials.** This is probably the best proof you can offer.

■ **Use precise numbers.** People are convinced more by precise numbers than rounded numbers.

■ **Use the power of print.** Printed supporting evidence, from publications such as books and magazines that support your case, is persuasive.

Street Talk

One can stand as the greatest orator the world has known, possess the quickest mind, employ the cleverest psychology, and have mastered all the technical devices of argument, but if one is not credible one might just as well preach to the pelicans.

GERRY SPENCE
LEADING TRIAL LAWYER AND AUTHOR

Communicate Your Position

Set the Bargaining Range
Wherever possible seasoned negotiators try to avoid stating their opening positions until they have had a chance to fully discuss the other side's needs. Once you present your opening position, it's hard to avoid haggling over positions, especially where price is an issue.

> He who mentions the first number loses
>
> NEGOTIATOR'S MAXIM

Where it makes sense to disclose your opening position early you need to be prepared. If you have done your homework, you should have prepared an ambitious yet credible proposal.

Discover Their Position
If possible, get the other side to make the first offer. Most people provide far more information than they need to. They sometimes reveal their priorities, and every so often they offer more than you ever dreamed of asking for. Very likely, the person on the other side will also be asking for more than they expect to get. So don't be too dismayed if initially the differences between the opening positions seem large.

Smart Tips & Tactics

- **Keep your opening proposals brief and to the point.** Don't provide too many details, or they may be used against you in a counter proposal.

- **Look the other person straight in the eye when you present your opening position.** Speak calmly and confidently.

- **Avoid vague tentative phrases such as:**
  - We would like to get *about* . . .
  - We are looking for a price *in the range of* . . .
  - As a *first offer* we were hoping for . . .

- **After you've stated your position, go quiet.** Then wait for their reaction.

- **If the other side makes the first offer, don't immediately counter offer.** Question them further to get more information before replying.

StreetTalk

How much should you ask for? Start by asking for the best terms you can justify . . . with a straight face. First, you can't expect to conclude a negotiation without making concessions. Second, your opponent needs to participate in the outcome. Third, by setting high goals, you're more likely to achieve them. Finally, it's the way of the world.

MARC DIENER
DEALMAKER, BUSINESS ATTORNEY, AND AUTHOR[1]

50

Create a Positive Nonverbal Climate

> A negotiator should observe everything. You must be part Sherlock Holmes, part Sigmund Freud
>
> Victor Kiam
> COMPANY DIRECTOR

Forming Your First Impression
- When we meet someone for the first time we:
  - First, scan their face and eyes.
  - Second, look at their body.
  - Third, examine what they are wearing.
  - Fourth, listen to their tone of voice.
  - Fifth, if appropriate, shake their hands.
  - Sixth, listen to their words.

Meeting Face to Face
The opening discussions set the tone and climate for the rest of the negotiation. In a typical negotiation we spend 90 percent of the time discussing—talking, listening and watching each other.

The Impact of Body Language
We are perceived three ways:
- Visually (body language)
- Vocally (tone of voice)
- Verbally (spoken words)

The tone of the opening discussions is largely determined by nonverbal signals. So, when our body talk and words contradict each other, people believe the body talk.

Smart Tips & Tactics

■ **Face your opposite number squarely.** Most people focus on your face as their cue to gauge your attitude, feelings and emotional state.

■ **Assume an open posture.** When you sit with legs uncrossed and slightly apart, you convey warmth and openness. Open hands also signal that you are sincere and open to new ideas.

■ **Lean forward.** When you lean forward in a chair towards the other party with your hands on your knees, you are indicating interest. You are also showing you are listening and are ready to proceed.

■ **Maintain eye contact.** If you want to communicate interest and empathy, look the other person in the eye.

■ **Relax.** A comfortable, relaxed, yet attentive pose lets the other person know you're ready to listen.

StreetTalk

First impressions can undoubtedly mislead us. Both Winston Churchill and Neville Chamberlain didn't take Adolf Hitler seriously at first. Why? Hitler's posturing, absurd little mustache and slicked-down hair made him look stupid. In the same way Bill Gates was probably underrated by some of his early competitors because of his "nerd" or "geek" appearance.

HARRY MILLS
ARTFUL PERSUASION[2]

Influence with Questions

> There are two sides to every question, your own side, and the wrong side.
>
> SYDNEY J. HARRIS
> NEWSPAPER COLUMNIST

Question, Question, Question

Questions are among the most potent communication tools negotiators can use. All negotiators must know how and when to ask questions and use them to control the direction and pace of a meeting, negotiation or sale. Neil Rackham of the Huthwaite Research Group found "skilled negotiators ask more than twice as many questions as average negotiators."

Questions Persuade

Successful negotiators use questions to plant ideas in the other party's mind, and then get them to nurture their ideas as if they were their own. Whereas questions move negotiations forward, statements often create roadblocks to be navigated around.

Questions Keep You in Control

Questions give you power to control the content, tone, pace and direction of a negotiation. With questions you can control the issues you want to discuss—and also what you want to avoid. With questions you can set the mood and tone of a negotiation, you can slow down or force the pace of a discussion.

Smart Tips & Tactics

- **When you prepare, list all the questions you don't have answers to.** Every question you don't know the answer to is a potential trap.

- **Avoid questions that:**
  - *Accuse.* Was it you coming back from lunch at 2:30 pm?
  - *Entrap.* Are you still beating your wife?
  - *Force agreement.* This is the best deal—don't you agree?
  - *Threaten.* How do you expect more business, given your lousy service?

- **Use these questions to build cooperation:**
  - What do you see as our areas of common interest?
  - Are there any particular areas where you feel I'm being inflexible?
  - Is there another way we could more productively tackle this issue?
  - Is there anything that I haven't clarified to your satisfaction?

Ask questions to which you already know the answers. You may learn more from their wrong answers than their right ones.

MARC DIENER
DEALMAKER, BUSINESS ATTORNEY, AND AUTHOR[3]

Listen to Advantage

Persuasive Listening
A major survey of negotiators involving over 5,000 participants found negotiators fail to identify shared priorities about half of the time. Poor questioning and listening lies at the heart of many of these failures.

Give Your Total Attention
Questions are useless if you don't listen carefully to the response. The best way to get a person to tell you more is to show the person that you are listening. If you listen actively—give the person your total attention and respond to what they say—they will soon loosen up.

Create Empathy
Actively listening will help you empathize with the other person. To have empathy with someone does not mean to sympathize. To emphathize means to understand, to see through the eyes of another.

> Nature has given to men one tongue, but two ears, that we may hear from others twice as much as we speak.
>
> EPICTETUS
> GREEK PHILOSOPHER

Smart Tips & Tactics

- **Paraphrase content with phrases such as:**
  - It sounds like . . .
  - In other words . . .
  - So, . . .
  - So what you're saying . . .
  - It seems that . . .

- **Wait for the other person to confirm the accuracy of your paraphrase.** Remember, paraphrases are tentative. You don't know your interpretation is correct until the other person replies, "Yes that's it!"

- **Acknowledge and accept feelings.** When you acknowledge feelings by labeling and accepting them, you deepen rapport.

- **Don't interrupt—even when you strongly disagree with the other side.** Interruption destroys rapport.

Street Talk

Act Dumb: *"Pretend you know less than you do, and your opponent may tell you more than you need."* This is what one top negotiator calls the Columbo technique, where you act like such an ignoramus that the criminal in his arrogance practically hands you himself on a platter.

LEONARD KOREN AND PETER GOODMAN, *THE HAGGLER'S HANDBOOK*[4]

Use Persuasive Language

> The real message isn't what you say. It's what the other person remembers.
>
> HARRY MILLS
> *ARTFUL PERSUASION*

If your body language and voice are congruent, the other party will listen to the words you speak.

Use Assertive Language
Effective negotiators use assertive rather than aggressive or passive language to state clearly what they want, feel and think.

Aggressive speakers' words put people down. When attacked by aggressive speakers, we often take their words personally and counter in kind. Passive speakers, on the other hand, communicate submissiveness and docility through their words and thereby weaken any position they are trying to present.

In contrast, assertive speakers choose words which convey strength and authority. Assertive speakers put themselves forward without ever putting the other person down. They speak clearly and directly.

Aggressive	Assertive
What's the matter, can't you organize yourself? You're not managing very well.	I want you to schedule your time so the production staff are all assigned their daily jobs by 9:00 A.M.

Smart Tips & Tactics

■ **Use strong words.** If you feel strongly about something, use words to match. "This is the best way" is much better than "I think this is the best way."

■ **Leave out intensifiers.** Intensifiers like very, definitely and surely do the opposite of what they are supposed to do.

■ **Avoid fillers.** Powerless speakers use excessive pleases and thank-yous. Over politeness conveys timidity and uncertainty.

■ **Avoid weak statements such as:**
  ■ You may not agree with me but . . .
  ■ This may be what you're thinking, however . . .
  ■ I'm not 100 percent certain but . . .

Keep "demand" out of your vocabulary. When I am negotiating I never make demands. I never lay down ultimatums. The word "demand" is not in my vocabulary. . . .

Bob Wolff,
PROFESSIONAL NEGOTIATOR
AUTHOR[5]

Words That Sell

Words Evoke Emotions
Top negotiators choose their words with great precision. The right words can move people to agreement. The wrong words can result in deadlock and animosity.

Warm and Cold Words
There are warm words and cold words just as there are warm and cold colors. Warm words help us feel safe and secure. Cold words create doubt and unease. Cold words have their place, but use them with care.

Warm	**Cold**
- Agree	- Abnormal
- Approval	- Afraid
- Basic	- Cannot
- Care	- Disagree
- Fair	- Disappoint
- Fresh	- Fruitless
- Fun	- Nonsense
- Good	- Ruthless
- Hope	- Underhand
- Independent	- Unfair
- New	- Unfortunately
- Sincere	- Warning

Persuasive Words

Here is a list of some persuasive words in the English language. Use them to persuade and convince.

Appealing	Moving
Authentic	New
Comfortable	Notable
Comprehensive	Original
Convenient	Peace of mind
Discovery	Positive
Easy	Promise
Gain	Proven
Generous	Reduce
Genuine	Reliable
Guarantee	Results
Have	Safe
Improve	Save
Increase	Security
Influential	Simplifies
Legitimate	Straightforward
Love	Tested
Memorable	Unique
Money	Versatile

Use Silence for Advantage

The Power of Silence
Most negotiators don't give the other side enough time to think. If you jump in too early, the other side becomes defensive and less cooperative.

Silence creates pressure. Top negotiators will tell you if you want to uncover what is happening, don't fill the silences in a conversation. The other side will begin to feel awkward and uncomfortable and then fill in the gaps. They will usually tell you everything you want to hear.

Silence as a Weapon
Adversarial negotiators often use silence as a weapon when asked tricky questions. First they go quiet, then they stare straight at the other party's eyes. Often the other part is unsettled enough to give up on the question and go on to the next point.

Silence on the Phone
Silence works particularly well on the phone. The other party often feels compelled to fill in the silences with concessions or valuable information.

> I have never been hurt by anything I didn't say.
>
> CALVIN COOLIDGE
> 30TH PRESIDENT OF THE UNITED STATES

Smart Tips & Tactics

■ **Stop talking and stay silent until the other side speaks, immediately after you have:**
- presented a proposal
- summarized progress
- asked a question
- reached agreement.

■ **Don't rush in with the answer when the other side presents a proposal.** Pause and hold back your reply. Many people can't stand the silence and throw in an extra concession to break it.

■ **In team negotiations spell out who will do the talking.** If a team member can't stay quiet, consider removing him.

■ **Don't interrupt.** Always stay quiet when the other party is talking. Never interrupt. It upsets the speaker, and upset speakers concede less.

Street Talk

A young Thomas Edison, having invented a stock ticker, traveled to New York to sell the patent rights to some businessmen. Edison decided that he was going to ask for $5,000 for the invention, but would settle for $3,000. When he got to the meeting he was so intimidated by the potential buyers and their trappings that he could hardly speak. After some time had passed, one of the businessmen broke the silence and offered $40,000. Edison was stunned but found his voice in time to accept the offer.

Translate the Meta-Talk

> When you say one thing, the clever person understands three.
>
> CHINESE PROVERB

What is Meta-Talk?
When we uses meta-talk, as it is called, we say one thing and mean another. Meta-talk is part and parcel of every negotiation.

Here are some examples of meta-talk:
- Don't take this as criticism . . .
- As you are well aware . . .
- Although I've been given full authority to settle . . .
- We think this is most fair and reasonable . . .
- I hear what you say but . . .
- In my humble opinion . . .

Meta-Talk Increases Conflict
Meta-talk irritates, annoys and derails negotiations. When the other party says "I think you'll find this offer more than generous," they are in effect saying, "I'm doing you a big favor and if you reject this offer or try to modify it, you are unfair, unreasonable or selfish."

Avoid Meta-Talk
Research shows skilled negotiators use meta-talk far less than average negotiators.

Smart Tips & Tactics

■ **Listen for double meanings.** Watch out for these troublesome meta-words or phrases. They all signal deceit:
- Incidentally...
- By the way...
- While I think of it...
- Frankly...
- Honestly...
- Sincerely...

■ **Don't use words such as fair, reasonable and generous.** They irritate and offend.

■ **Check out others' meta-talk when you suspect someone.** Repeat the words in your mind, listening to the way each word is emphasized.

■ **If meta-talk is fouling the negotiation raise it as a separate issue.** Most negotiators don't appreciate the damage it creates.

Hidden Meanings:
Statements that start "Don't be concerned, but..." or "You have nothing to worry about..." mean only one thing. There is something to be worried about.

ROBERT MAYER,
ATTORNEY, AUTHOR AND DEALMAKER[6]

R-E-S-P-E-C-T

The seven steps to agreement

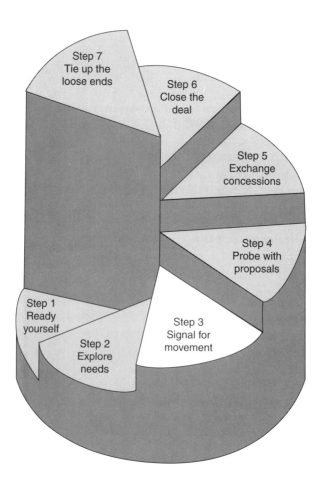

Chapter Four

STEP 3 SIGNAL FOR MOVEMENT

The journey of 1000 miles starts with a single step.
　　Chinese Proverb

Features
In Step Three you: **Signal** for movement. Here you:

- Signal that you are prepared to move.
- Respond to signals from the other side and build momentum.

How to Signal

The Purpose of Signaling

Negotiations often start out with both sides taking strong, seemingly immovable opening positions. The opening statements are strong, unconditional and unqualified. For example: One party initially declares: "It is *impossible* to change our delivery schedule."

After some discussion the negotiator signals he is willing to modify his opening position by saying: "We would find it *extremely difficult* to meet that schedule." He has sent a signal.

Subtle Changes

The original, absolute message has been qualified. This message, indicating a willingness to move, is called a signal. Signals allow negotiators to move from their opening position without giving an impression to the other negotiator that they are about to cave in.

Signals normally precede proposals but they crop up whenever negotiators lock over positions.

Listen Intently

Most people miss signals because they are not listening properly. The result can be prolonged argument. Because signals are, by definition, subtle changes in language, they are easily missed.

> The fellow that agrees with everything you say is either a fool or he is getting ready to skin you.
>
> Frank McKinney (Kin) Hubbard
> American humorist

Smart Tips & Tactics

■ *To signal your willingness to move, simply add qualifications to your statements.* For example:
- We do not *normally* give credit.
- We cannot meet *all* of your needs.

These should generate replies such as:
- Under what circumstances do you give credit?
- Which request can you meet?

■ **Clarify all signals with follow-up questions.**
For example:
- Could you clarify when you could change your schedule?
- Under what conditions would you be willing to make a deposit?

■ **Reward their signals by reciprocating with your own signals.**

■ **Repeat or reword missed signals.**
Signals are often missed or misunderstood.

A signal addresses the common problem negotiators face when they are inhibited from moving through fear of giving in and of sliding down the slippery slope to surrender.

GAVIN KENNEDY
AUTHOR OF NINE BOOKS ON NEGOTIATION
BUSINESS SCHOOL PROFESSOR AND
FREELANCE NEGOTIATING SKILLS SPECIALIST[1]

R-E-S-P-E-C-T
The seven steps to agreement

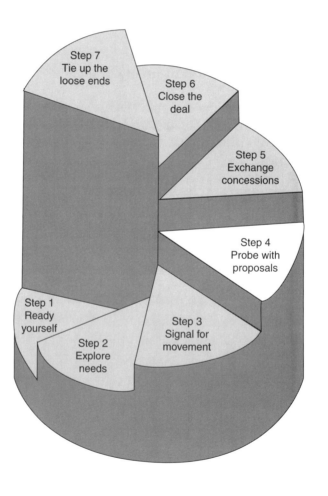

Chapter Five

STEP 4 PROBE WITH PROPOSALS

Successful collaborative negotiation lies in finding out what the other side really wants and showing them a way to get it, while you get what you want.

> HERB COHEN
> AUTHOR, AND SPEAKER
> DESCRIBED BY PLAYBOY MAGAZINE
> AS THE WORLD'S BEST NEGOTIATOR

Features
In Step Four you: **Probe** with proposals. To advance the negotiation you:

- Make tentative proposals in order to probe for points where the other side will make concessions.

- Repackage rejected proposals into a more acceptable form.

Use Proposals to Generate Movement

Once a positive signal has been received, negotiations move to the proposal phase. Here both sides probe for areas of further movement by putting up proposals, or tentative suggestions to address their needs and concerns.

What Is a Proposal?

It is important to remember that a proposal is a tentative suggestion for resolving differences. It is *not* a specific offer to bargain. For example, a negotiator might propose:

"If you will increase the discount, then we'll consider raising our minimum order."

Here the negotiator is being deliberately tentative. He is using the minimum order to elicit information, and generate movement.

Proposals Create Flexibility

By clarifying the priorities of both sides, proposals and counter proposals move negotiators one step closer to agreement.

Because proposals are merely tentative suggestions, they give negotiators greater flexibility when they later need to shift positions.

> Extremists think 'communication' means agreeing with them.
> LEO ROSTEN
> WRITER

Smart Tips & Tactics

- **Keep all proposals conditional.** State your condition first and be specific.
    - Use the if/then technique.
    - *If* you will cut your price by $60,000, *then* we will consider increasing the size of the order.
    - *If* you will increase sick leave to seven days, *then* we will look at our claim for medical insurance.

- **Remember, proposals give away information about your settlement range.** This is why your proposal is explicit about what you want the other side to do and vague about what you are prepared to do.

- **Keep your proposals brief.** Then go quiet until the other side replies. Long proposals can reveal too much about your priorities.

StreetTalk

Remember the two choice rule. When you want people to make a choice quickly, offer them two alternatives, either of which would be comfortable for you. They are more likely to reach a decision now when offered two alternatives.

KARE ANDERSON
AUTHOR AND EXPERT ON NEGOTIATION AND PERSUASION.
AUTHOR OF GETTING WHAT YOU WANT[1]

Package Your Proposals

Creating Options
Proposals allow both sides to plot out the key variables in the negotiation and determine each other's priorities. In a typical negotiation, lots of proposals end up on the table. Some are incompatible, but others overlap or complement each other. By juggling and reshuffling proposals you can often repackage them into a mutually acceptable parcel.

Multiply the Variables
Effective negotiators try to multiply the number of variables under discussion, as each additional variable creates more options for packaging. The more variables, the less likelihood there is of deadlock. The more variables, the better the chance of a win-win agreement.

Be Creative
Packaging calls for creativity, flexibility and patience. The trick is to find a package that addresses both sides' interests by trading what is cheap for you for what is valuable to the other side.

> If you have an important point to make, don't try to be subtle or clever. Hit the point once, then come back and hit it again. Then hit it a third time with a tremendous whack.
>
> WINSTON CHURCHILL
> STATESMAN AND PRIME MINISTER OF BRITAIN

Smart Tips & Tactics

■ **Never interrupt a counter proposal.** Interruptions antagonize the speaker who may tag a concession on at the end.

■ **Don't instantly reject a proposal.** Above all, avoid the proposal killer "I disagree."

■ **Try not to say no.** A "no" strangles discussion and halts movement.

■ **Don't immediately counter with your own proposal.** The worst time to present a counter proposal is just after the other side has put their proposal.

■ **Give as detailed a response as possible.** Also, indicate areas where agreement might be possible.

■ **Regularly summarize where you are at.** It creates a feeling of progress.

StreetTalk

To avoid getting stuck in a futile debate . . . try this formula whenever you need to reject a portion of a proposal:

*"I know just how you **feel**."*
*"In fact, I **felt** that way myself."*
*"But let me tell you what I **found**."*

ERIC WM. SKOPEC AND LAREE S. KIELY
BUSINESS STRATEGISTS AND ADVISORS[2]

R-E-S-P-E-C-T
The seven steps to agreement

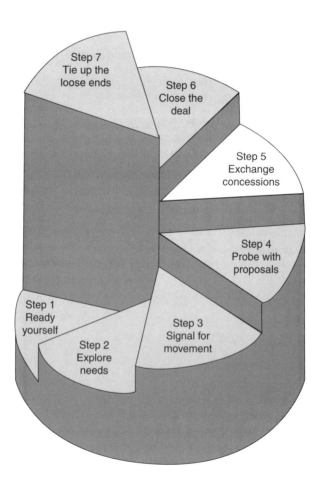

Chapter Six

STEP 5 EXCHANGE CONCESSIONS

An actor, negotiating a contract with movie mogul Sam Goldwyn, demanded "fifteen hundred a week." "You're not asking fifteen hundred a week," snapped back Goldwyn, "you're asking twelve hundred and I'm giving you a thousand."

Features
In Step Five you: **Exchange** concessions. Here you:

- Trade concessions by giving the other party some, or part, of their demands in exchange for receiving some, or part, of what you want.

- Aim high.

- Make credible offers.

- Concede slowly.

- Make sure the other side reciprocates.

- Track all concessions.

Trade for Advantage

> I make him an offer he can't refuse.
>
> MARIO PUZO, AUTHOR, *THE GODFATHER*

Trading

So far we've gone through the steps of preparing, communicating our opening positions and exploring both sides' needs. We've signaled our willingness to move and probed with proposals to find areas of possible agreement. Now we're ready to get down to trading—or exchanging—concessions.

Cost Every Concession

Before even making a concession ask yourself:
- What value is the concession to the other party?
- What will it cost me?
- What do I need in return?

Don't forget the *could get, should get, must get* framework you used while preparing to determine your objectives. The basis of successful bargaining is to trade your *could gets* (low priorities) so you can get your *must gets* (high priorities).

Before you start trading concessions, get all of the other party's demands on the table. Then make it clear that any concession on any one item is conditional upon agreement on the other outstanding issues.

Smart Tips & Tactics

- **Make all concessions conditional.** To protect yourself from giving away free concessions, preface all your offers with a condition. Use the if/then formula:
    - If you will increase your discount to 42.5 percent, then I will pay within seven days.

- **Justify all concessions.** Don't give away concessions without a plausible explanation as to why you are prepared to make concessions in this instance.

- **Track all concessions.** As you keep track of all the offers and concessions, patterns should emerge which reveal insights into the other party's priorities.

- **Calculate the relative concession rates.** By calculating the relative speeds of your and the other party's concession rates, you can get a good idea of how you are progressing.

Street Talk

Don't keep score on things that don't matter. In the heat of the deal, people sometimes ask for concessions just because they can. Resist this urge, which will only distract you from the bigger picture and eat up precious time. It can also make you look like a jerk.

LEO HINDERY, JR.
ARCHITECT OF OVER 240 BUSINESS DEALS WORTH OVER $150 BILLION
AUTHOR OF *THE BIGGEST GAME OF ALL*[1]

Open First?

> Ultimatum: A last demand before resorting to concessions.
>
> AMBROSE BIERCE,
> AUTHOR
> *THE DEVIL'S DICTIONARY*

Never Make the First Offer?

Lots of battle-hardened negotiators are adamant, "Never make the first offer." He who mentions the first offer loses.

Every negotiator has a tale of a negotiator who asked for too little. Beatles manager George Epstein cost his clients a fortune when he asked the producers of *A Hard Day's Night* for just 7.5 percent of the movies profits. The producers were prepared to pay 25 percent.

Anchoring the Deal

However, research shows negotiators who open first actually enjoy an advantage. Psychologically the first offer becomes an anchor or reference point, often causing the other side to rethink their demands. Opening first allows you to set the range of offers. Indeed, no other factor impacts more on the shape of the final deal than the first offer. So plan your opening offer with great care.

Smart Tips & Tactics

■ **Open first, if you believe you have better information than your opponent.** Your opening will often cause the other part to revise their expectations.

■ **Let the other party go first if you have serious doubts about your information.** Then ask them to justify their offer.

■ **If they open first, beware of being overly influenced by the anchoring effect.** Most negotiators unconsciously adjust their expectations towards their opening number.

■ **Once you've made your initial offer go silent.** Wait for the other side to respond before making a further concession.

■ **Counter-offer quickly if the other party opens.** This reduces the chance of being anchored by their initial offer. Plus, it shows you're willing to negotiate.

Street Talk

While building his American Tobacco trust, James B. Duke summoned R.J. Reynolds, a competitor, to his hotel room. "I'll give you one million for two-thirds of your company," Duke told Reynolds, "or I'll break you. Take your choice." Reynolds replied: "My price is three million. Otherwise for every dollar you cost me, I'm going to cost American Tobacco a hundred." Reynolds got his three million.

Open High?

How should you open? Should you open aggressively and pitch high, or should you start with a fair and reasonable offer.

Relationship Focus
If you want to build long-term relationship you should open with a fair and reasonable offer. Aggressive opening pitches can easily antagonize the other side and undermine the changes of any win-win arrangement.

> He who owns the most when he dies wins.
>
> Ivan Boesky
> financier

Bottom-Line Focus
If the relationship is unimportant, and the bottom line is all important, then it pays to play hardball: Open high and concede slowly. This doesn't mean you should ask for the moon. You still have to be credible. A credible offer is one that can be logically supported and justified.

Research shows, negotiators who start high end up with more of the final pie than those who start with lower aspirations. Negotiators typically judge their success by how much they move their opponent from their opening figure. Negotiators who start high have more room to move.

Smart Tips & Tactics

■ **Don't open high where you have a weak BATNA and the other side knows it.** You're simply inviting the other side to expose your weak hand.

■ **Don't highball, where the other party hates haggling.** Research shows 15 percent of Americans detest haggling and won't do business with hardball negotiators.

■ **Don't be afraid to open high in a relationship-based negotiation,** where your ambitious proposal can be backed by solid, credible evidence.

■ **Making concessions is not a sign of weakness.** Rational concessions show the other side that you accept the legitimacy of their demands.

> *Research confirms that people receiving concessions often feel better about the bargaining process than people who get a single, "fair" price. In fact, they feel better even when they end up paying more than they otherwise might.*
>
> G. RICHARD SHELL
> DIRECTOR OF THE WHARTON EXECUTIVE
> NEGOTIATION WORKSHOP
> BARGAINING FOR ADVANTAGE[2]

Beware the Gender Trap

> When women go wrong, men go right after them.
>
> MAE WEST
> ACTRESS

Research shows women negotiate in ways that disadvantage them. Linda Babcock, who teaches negotiation at Carneigie Mellon University, says women as a whole do worse in negotiations because of the way they negotiate.

Women Don't Like to Negotiate
According to Babcock, women don't like to negotiate. Two and a half times more women than men say they feel "a great deal of apprehension" about negotiating. When asked to choose a metaphor for negotiations, men picked 'winning a ball game,' while women picked 'going to the dentist.'

Women Don't Ask
The biggest mistake women make is they don't negotiate and ask for more when going for a job or buying a car. For example, when it comes to settling their first salary package, just 7 percent of women haggle over their salary, compared to 57 percent of males who ask for more. As a result male graduates earn an average 7.6 percent of $4,000 more than female students. By not negotiating over salary an individual stands to lose over $500,000 by age 60.

Rather than haggle over a car, women will pay as much as $1,353 more.

Exchange Concessions

Smart Tips & Tactics

■ **Identify low-risk areas such as a local market where you can practice asking for more.** Take a deep breath and be assertive when making requests.

■ **Ask for 30 percent more than you confidently expect to get.** You'll be surprised how often the other party accepts.

■ **Practice verbalizing your opening out loud in front of the mirror.** This is a useful exercise to build up confidence.

■ **Develop a credible case to support each of your demands.** A well-developed case will dramatically improve your odds of a successful negotiation.

Men initiate negotiations about four times more often than women. Women are more pessimistic about the rewards available, and so come away with an average 30 percent less when they negotiate. Twenty percent of women say they never negotiate, even when negotiation is appropriate and necessary.

LINDA BABCOCK AND SARA LASCHEVES
AUTHORS, *WOMEN DON'T ASK: NEGOTIATION AND THE GENDER DIVIDE*[3]

Slicing the Pie

One-Time Transactions
Transaction-driven negotiators view negotiation as a win-lose contest—as one-off events. They win, you lose. Transaction-driven negotiators are essentially hagglers where price concerns dominate.

Start High, Concede Slowly
One "experiment" compared three different concession strategies:

1. Start high, then refuse to move
2. Start moderately, then refuse to move
3. Start high, then gradually concede to the moderate point.

Strategy (3) was by far the most successful. Negotiators closed more deals, made more money per deal, and their opponents were much happier with their agreements than with negotiators who refused to move.

Making the First Move
It also pays to avoid making the first major concession. Research shows that losers generally make the first concessions on major issues. Skilled negotiators, if they have to make the first concession to get momentum going, make it on a minor issue.

> My style of dealmaking is quite simple and straightforward. I just keep pushing and pushing to get what I'm after.
>
> DONALD TRUMP
> PROPERTY DEVELOPER AND CASINO OPERATOR

Smart Tips & Tactics

■ **Manage your concession size and pattern.** Signal you are reaching your limit by sharply cutting the size of your concessions.

■ **Trade reluctantly.** Make the other side work for every concession.

■ **Make a series of small concessions.** Avoid making large concessions.

■ **Be patient—concede slowly.** Negotiators who move too fast easily lose control.

■ **Conserve your concessions.** Hold some concessions in reserve for last-minute demands.

■ **Demand reciprocation.** Never make a concession without getting a concession in return.

■ **Avoid tit-for-tat concessions.** Don't fall into the trap of matching the other side's concessions.

■ **Be wary of split-the-differences offers.** Before you agree to any such offer calculate where the split will occur and where this fits with your settlement range.

I wanted a new TV. My wife wanted a new car, so we compromised. We got the TV but we keep it in the garage.

ANONYMOUS

Enlarging the Pie

Relationship-Based Negotiations
Relationship-focused negotiators look for a long-term relationship so they can expand the pie and build win-win agreements. To enlarge the pie you need to identify tradeables that can be dovetailed together to satisfy the interests of both parties. To enlarge the pie you need to identify tradeables that are cheap for you and valuable for the other side.

Exploit Your Differences
The most valuable tradeables come from your differences:
- *Different interests.* What do you care about that is not important to them?
- *Different beliefs.* How might you dovetail differences in your beliefs?
- *Different resources.* What different assets can you trade?
- *Different valuations.* What things are valuable to you but of little value to them?
- *Different forecasts.* What different views about the chances of a future event occurring do you hold?
- *Different attitudes to risk.* Do you have different capacities? Is one party more risk averse?
- *Different time preferences.* Do you have different short-term and long-term needs? Do you have different deadlines?

> Without common interests there is nothing to negotiate for; without conflicting interests there is nothing to negotiate about.
>
> F.C. IKLÉ
> AUTHOR, *HOW NATIONS NEGOTIATE*

Smart Tips & Tactics

■ **Multiply the variables.** Increasing the number of issues or tradeables dramatically increases the odds of a win-win agreement.

■ **Adopt a moderate opening position.** Start with a credible, realistic offer based on objective criteria.

■ **Negotiate the total package.** Don't allow your negotiation to become a series of separate, single issue offers and trades.

■ **Offer multiple options simultaneously.** Offering a range of "equal value" options increases cooperation.

■ **Ask for preferences and priorities.** Only 7 percent of untrained negotiators ever bother to ask the other party what their preferences are.

■ **Treat distributive issues as a shared problem.** Where possible negotiate procedures to resolve differences in advance.

*Jack Sprat could eat no fat,
His wife could eat no lean;
So 'twixt' them both they
cleared the cloth and licked
the platter clean.*

MOTHER GOOSE NURSERY RHYME

Build Momentum

Prevent Deadlock
Momentum can easily be lost in a negotiation, degenerating into deadlock.

Emphasize Shared Interests
Continually emphasize the common interests of both sides. As tension increases both sides tend to exaggerate their differences and play down their similarities.

Summarize Progress
Regularly summarize the progress you have made. Some negotiators even set time aside during a negotiation to critique how they are doing. This time can be used to review the ground rules, procedures and negotiator behavior.

Stay Flexible
Constantly state your willingness to trade. Cultivate a reputation for being flexible as well as tough.

Multiply the Issues
Slice large issues that are likely to cause deadlock into smaller, easier-to-manage pieces. The more issues you have to trade, the greater the chances of a win-win agreement.

> If there is any one secret of success, it lies in the ability to get the other person's point of view and see things from that person's angle as well as from your own.
>
> HENRY FORD
> AUTOMOBILE MANUFACTURER

Smart Tips & Tactics

■ **Reward concessions.** When the other side grants a concession, say "I appreciate that" rather than "that's not good enough."

■ **Avoid making statements such as "This is my final offer."** This effectively says to the other side, "Take it or leave it."

■ **Don't turn minor issues into matters of principle.** Backing down then involves a loss of face.

■ **Shift issues at impasses.** If you are getting bogged down, shift issues.

■ **Handle the ridiculous offer with care.** Rather than storm out, stay calm and polite.

Lost Opportunities: In an analysis of 32 negotiation research studies involving 5,000 people, researchers found negotiators failed to identify shared interests about 50 percent of the time.

LEIGH THOMPSON,
AUTHOR, *THE MIND AND HEART OF THE NEGOTIATOR*[4]

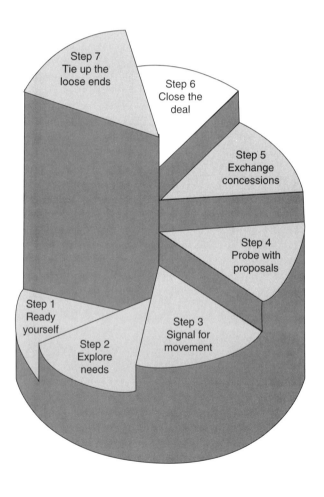

Chapter Seven

STEP 6 CLOSE THE DEAL

I always win. You always lose. What could be fairer than that.
    Ashleigh Brilliant

Features
In Step six you: **Close** the deal. To end the bargaining process you:

- Look for closing cues.
- Make a credible and acceptable close.
- Start with a summary close.

Manage the Tension

Keep Your Cool
The closing step is tense. Both sides are close to their limit as deadlines loom closer. Fear of deadlock increases. Patience is wearing thin, nerves give way and mistakes are made.

Stay in Control
To escape tension, some negotiators simply walk away and abandon potentially good deals. Others become aggressive and belligerent, making ridiculous stands on minor issues of principle.

Watch for Deadline Pressure
Keep referring to your time plan. Keep smiling and project confidence through your body language. Remember, most large concessions are conceded at the "eleventh hour" when negotiators feel their negotiating leverage crumble as their deadline looms ever closer. It is therefore imperative you keep your cool, stay calm and remain vigilant.

Walk Away if Necessary
Keep reminding yourself what your BATNA is. Sometimes the best deals are the ones we had the courage to walk away from.

> Eighty percent of us believe that we are in the top 10 percent of how well we get along with others.
>
> 1989 GALLUP POLL

Smart Tips & Tactics

■ **Don't get rattled by the fear of deadlock.** The more time we invest in a negotiation, the more we have to lose from a breakdown.

■ **Try to anticipate, avoid or sidestep last-minute deadlocks.** Be prepared to add extra tradeables.

■ **Change the time scale.** If the negotiation is bogging down over short-term issues, stress the long-term benefits of agreement.

■ **Change the negotiator if necessary.** Sometimes a new face is needed.

■ **Consider a mediator.** An independent third party can work wonders.

Street Talk

Listening is far more effective than arguing as a way to resolve conflict. A good listener is like an engineer dealing with a river that floods after a heavy rain. Only a fool would try to defeat gravity by attempting to push the river back upstream. The wise engineer makes gravity her friend. She builds a canal and holding ponds at the proper place and lets the water flow of its own accord.

BRIAN MULDOON
PROFESSIONAL MEDIATOR AND EXPERT IN
ALTERNATIVE DISPUTE RESOLUTION
AUTHOR, *THE HEART OF CONFLICT* [1]

94

When to Close

> A. B. C.
> Always Be Closing.
> OLD SELLER'S MAXIM

Commitment
You've been making concessions. So has the other side. But now you're getting close to your limit. How do you bring the negotiation to an end?

Watch for Body Language Clues
Judging when to close is always difficult. Start by looking for signals in the body language of the other party.

The chief executive of a foodstore chain, sitting arms crossed with locked ankles, uncrosses his legs and leans forward in the chair and moves closer to the senior partner of a legal firm who is presenting a proposal to take over the company's legal services.

These changes in body talk can be signals that the chief executive is close to agreement or has made up his mind.

Listen for Clues
You listen for clues in the other party's words for indications that they are ready to close. If you are selling you would listen for questions such as:
- When can I get delivery?
- When do we have to pay for it?
- How could we extend the warranty from 18 months to two years?

These indicate the other side has actually mentally agreed and is ready to close.

Smart Tips & Tactics

When checking for signs of closure look out for the closing gestures:
- Warm smile
- Unfolded arms
- Leaning forward
- Relaxed body
- Unbuttoned/removed coat (for men)
- Direct eye contact with dilated pupils
- Open palms
- Alert facial expression
- Close proximity
- Sitting on edge of chair
- Nodding in agreement

Learn to Walk Away

One of the hardest things in business is to walk away from a deal that you really want. But sometimes it's the only way to get what you want or, ever important, what you need.

LEO HINDERY, JR.
CEO YES
ARCHITECT OF OVER 240 BUSINESS DEALS
WORTH OVER $150 BILLION[2]

The Summary Close

There are a variety of ways to successfully close a deal but I like to start with what is called the summary close.

In the summary close you close the negotiation by:
- Summarizing all that has been agreed to up till then.
- Emphasizing the concessions you have made.
- Highlighting the benefits of agreeing to your proposals.

Examples

Here is an example of a sales negotiation using a summary close to clinch a deal:

"So far we've agreed on the base price for the TR300 machine of $476,000 plus an installation fee of $78,000. That's a reduction of 18 percent off our normal price for that machine, while the installation fee has been cut by 27.5 percent."

"Once installed the TR300 will speed up your invoice processing by 16 percent. It's much easier to use than your present system so training time will be much less. You've also mentioned how it will improve cash flow by speeding up payments."

"Given the progress we've made it would be a shame if we now failed to reach agreement."

> To win one hundred victories in one hundred battles is not the acme of skill. To subdue the enemy without fighting is the acme of skill.
>
> SUN-TZU
> CHINESE STRATEGIST

Smart Tips & Tactics

■ **Look the other party straight in the eye when you close.** Be confident and assertive.

■ **Avoid the words "fair and reasonable" when you sum up your final offer.** These words irritate and annoy.

■ **Don't put previously agreed-to issues back on the table.** Stay focused on the issues that remain unresolved.

■ **If you're feeling rushed or anxious, slow down.** Agreements made in haste are often flawed.

Street Talk

Acknowledge Your Differences with Optimism

Expressing your agreement with your opponent does not mean suppressing your differences. Indeed, it is often helpful to acknowledge them openly. It assures your opponent that you have understood his side of the story, which helps him relax. In many ethnic conflicts, for example, the parties only feel comfortable acknowledging areas of agreement after they have clearly delineated the areas of disagreement.

WILLIAM URY
PROGRAM MEMBER ON NEGOTIATION AT HARVARD LAW SCHOOL
AUTHOR, *GETTING PAST NO*, AND CO-AUTHOR, *GETTING TO YES*[3]

Two More Proven Closes

> I can buy 20 percent of you or I can buy all of you. Or, I can go into this business myself and bury you.
>
> BILL GATES
> CHAIRMAN, MICROSOFT,
> TO STEVE CASE, CEO,
> AMERICA ONLINE (AOL)

Splitting the Difference

An offer to split the difference will often close a deal. If, for example, you are $10,000 apart, you will often get a better response to an offer to split the difference than you will to a concession of $5,000.

Splitting the difference works because it requires both sides to move and it appeals to our notions of equity.

The Weighing Close.

In this situation the other side seems keen on making a deal but still seems hesitant. To secure a close you say: "I appreciate you are very keen that any decision you make is the right one. So let's weight up the reasons for hesitating against the reasons for proceeding with the agreement now."

You then take a piece of paper and draw a line down the middle. On one side you get the other party to list the reasons why they are hesitant, on the other side you list the reasons for proceeding now.

Smart Tips & Tactics

■ **Use "split the difference" where issues of equity are important.** Splitting the difference appeals to our sense of fairness and encourages reciprocity.

■ **Avoid "split the difference" if the midpoint puts you at a disadvantage.** If you've opened moderately and the other side has opened aggressively the midpoint is likely to favor the other side.

■ **Use the weighing close with logic-driven personalities.** Logic-driven personalities like the mechanics of the weighing close.

■ **Try the weighing close when you need to get a procrastinator to say yes.** The weighing close can sometimes tip the scales from "maybe" to "yes."

Street Talk

Hire a Trusted Third Party

Where the gap between the two parties is too large or neither side is willing to play split the difference, another option is to hire a trusted go-between. In 1901, J.P. Morgan and the Rockefellers deadlocked over the sale of Mesabi ore fields because neither would offer a starting price. A trusted go-between, Henry Clay Frick, soothed both sides egos by working out a fair price ($80 million) which both sides could agree to.

100

Consider Contingent Contracts

Anticipating the Future

Lots of deals fail to close, turn sour, or fail because of differences between the parties over how they think the future will develop. One of the best ways to overcome differences caused by debate and uncertainty over what the future will bring, is to use a contingent contract.

> The trouble with our times is that the future is not what it used to be.
> PAUL VALERY
> FRENCH POET

What Is a Contingent Contract

When a software developer agrees to accept a lower up-front payment in return for an escalating royalty on future sales, he has entered into a *contingent* contract. It is a contingent contract because the terms don't take full effect until an uncertain event—in this case a future sales target, the contingency—takes place.

A contingent contract is ideal in these circumstances because it is not unusual for software developers to hold highly optimistic views about the likely future sales of their creations. It's also not unusual for buyers of software rights to be much more cautious.

Smart Tips & Tactics

■ **Use contingent contracts when you need to incentivize the other side to perform.** They work with salespeople, suppliers, CEOs and sports stars.

■ **Consider contingent contracts when you need to reduce risks.** Contingent contracts can give you the safety net you need to confidently close a deal.

■ **Consider contingent contracts when you need to test the honesty or true intentions of the other party.** Contingent contracts encourage party's to be open.

■ **Make sure the contingent contracts terms are clear and unambiguous.** Vague terms are always open to reinterpretation and manipulation.

Street Talk

Motivating Dennis Rodman to Perform

During the 1996 season, the Chicago Bulls basketball team owners paid out, to the talented but notoriously unpredictable Dennis Rodman, $2.96 million for 27 games he didn't even play. Rodman was guaranteed payment, regardless of whether he played. In 1997, the Bulls moved Rodman on to the most incentive-laden deal in National Basketball Association history. Rodman could earn $10.5 million if he met all the performance criteria, but he was guaranteed only $4.5 million. The contingent contract incentivized Rodman to perform. Rodman played 80 of a possible 82 games and collected $10.1 million of his possible $10.5 million salary. Plus, the Bulls won the championship.

MAX BAZERMAN AND JAMES J. GILLESPIE
AUTHORS, *BETTING ON THE FUTURE: THE VIRTUES OF CONTINGENT CONTRACTS*[4]

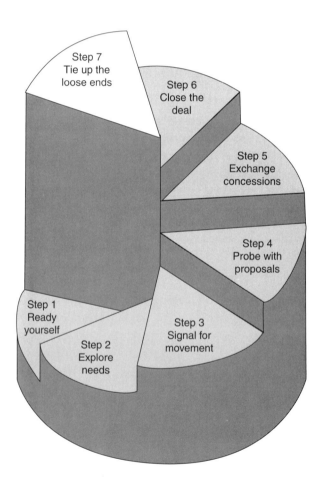

Chapter Eight

STEP 7 — TIE UP THE LOOSE ENDS

For want of a nail the shoe was lost;
For want of a shoe the horse was lost;
For want of a rider the battle was lost;
All for the want of care about a horseshoe nail.

    Benjamin Franklin

In Step Seven you: **Tie up** the loose ends. Here you:

- Confirm exactly what has been agreed.
- Summarize the details of the agreement on paper.
- Agree on a plan to settle possible future differences.

Verify What Has Been Agreed

Verify, Verify, Verify

Don't ever leave a negotiation until you have gone back over every point in the agreement. Check your understanding against theirs and clear up any problems of interpretation. If you can't agree on what was said and agreed at this stage, you are unlikely to do so later.

> The minute you read something you don't understand, you can almost be sure it was drawn up by a lawyer.
> WILL ROGERS
> COMEDIAN

Clarifying misunderstandings is much easier now as the memories of both sides are relatively fresh. Later, as memories fade, simple misunderstandings easily escalate into major differences as both sides start questioning each other's motives.

Draft Enforceable Agreements

Most dealmakers need professional help when it comes to drafting and advising on legally enforceable agreements.

Few dealmakers fully understand the legal obligations that flow from agreements in principle, memoranda of understanding or purchase and sale agreements. Nor do they appreciate what form of legal agreement best serves their interests as they move toward final closure.

Smart Tips & Tactics

■ **Take charge of the writing.** As the writer, you are forced to think about the exact meaning of every word and clause.

■ **Draw up a memo of understanding before separating.** Then get both sides to initial it.

■ **Have a lawyer check it out for potential legal fishhooks.** If the other side has their legal experts along for the closing, so should you.

■ **Write the agreement in plain explicit language.** Draft it so it cannot possibly be misunderstood.

■ **Anticipate future differences.** Plan for future meetings to resolve differences while they are still small.

Increasing the Chances of Commitment

In 1997 two of Wall Street's largest firms, Dean Witter Discover & Co. and the Morgan Stanley Group, announced they had agreed to merge. To increase the chances of the deal going through each firm promised to pay the other $250 million if it walked away from the deal.

Review Your Performance

While your memory is still fresh enough to recall what happened, review your performance. First, write down what happened in the order that it occurred. Second, go through each of the seven steps of the RESPECT model and assess your performance.

Ask questions such as:
- Did we identify all the key personalities and their constituents?
- Did we use our BATNA to maximum effect?
- Did we select the best team for the task?
- Did we identify their critical issues?
- Were we able to accurately prioritize their concerns?
- Did we identify potentially valuable trading opportunities?
- How successful was our concession plan?
- How well did our agenda management work?
- How well did our overall strategy work?
- Did our tactics support and reinforce our strategy?
- Did we make any wrong assumptions?
- How well did we manage our risks?

Judge your overall performance by answering the big questions:
- How well did we do?
- Where could we have done better?
- What can we do to improve our performance in future negotiations?

> Success is simply a matter of luck. Ask any failure.
>
> EARL WILSON
> NEWSPAPER COLUMNIST

PERFORMANCE REVIEW		
Criteria	✓ x	**Comments**
Selected right team		
Identified key influencers		
Used BATNA well		
Identified their interests		
Identified critical issues		
Prioritized their concerns		
Identified valuable trades		
Managed agenda		
Planned concessions		
Selected well strategy		
Used correct tactics		
Made correct assumptions		
Overall Performance		
How well did we do?		
How could we have done better?		
What can we do to improve our performance in future negotiations?		

Chapter Nine

WINNING TACTICS

I will tell you the mistake you are always making. . . . You draw up your plans the day before the battle, when you do not yet know your adversary's movements, or what positions you will have to occupy.
    Napoleon Bonaparte
    French Emperor and General

Features:
Tactics are the ploys you use to achieve your strategy.

- Choose tactics that reinforce your strategy.
- Anticipate the other side's tactical ploys.
- Counter and sidestep negative tactics.

Choose Your Tactics

Setting Objectives
Tactics are the gambits and ploys you use to achieve your strategy. Negotiation tactics have two main objectives:

- To strengthen your position in the other party's eyes.
- To alter the other party's view of their own position.

The more you can achieve these objectives the more likely the deal will suit you better. This does not mean that your opponent will necessarily be worse off. You may both win from a settlement that is different from either of your original proposals.

Negative Tactics
Lots of negotiators use negative tactics to induce their opponents to accept far less than they should. The purpose of negative tactics is to manipulate and cajole the other part into thinking the settlement under offer is the best possible. Before you can deal with negative tactics you have to be able to recognize them and know how they work.

> Send two dozen roses to Room 424 and put "Emily I love you" on the back of the bill.
>
> GROUCHO MARX
> COMEDIAN

Smart Tips & Tactics

There are four ways to counter or prevent negative tactics. Your choice depends upon your strategy and your BATNA.

1. **Frame the negotiation as a joint problem solving exercise.** Openly acknowledge your diffeences and ask for their advice.

2. **Ignore them.** Not responding to a threat or a hardball tactic can often deflate an aggressor.

3. **Discuss the negative tactics.** If you don't like the aggressive tactics of the other side, raise it as a separate issue. Then negotiate about how you want to negotiate proposed changes.

4. **Counter in kind.** The danger is emotions will escalate and the deal will collapse in acrimony.

StreetTalk

Real estate developer Donald Trump is well known for storming out of negotiations at critical moments. "You know Donald's going to get up and leave, you just don't know when," reports one anonymous participant. Once a tactic becomes predictable it loses most of its impact. Opponents quickly learn to adjust their tactics and strategies.

STEVEN CLICK AND RACHEL CROSON, AUTHORS, *REPUTATION IN NEGOTIATIONS*[1]

Nibble

> If you can't get a dinner, get a sandwich.
>
> NEGOTIATOR'S MAXIM

Buying a Suit
I have a friend who never buys a suit without nibbling for a tie or belt. He waits for the salesperson to start writing out the sales docket, then says, "You'll throw in a free tie, won't you?" The tactic invariably works. The other party is already committed to the close, and is unwilling to risk the whole deal for the sake of a nibble that is so tiny, compared to the rest of the deal.

Nibbling is Widespread
Buyers nibble by paying invoices late, by claiming rebates they are not entitled to and asking for extra services to be provided for nothing.

Sellers nibble by adding on unexpected extra charges, by delivering slightly more than ordered or by not providing promised services.

The Contrast Factor
The nibble works because it is small compared to the total deal. Contrasted with the total price, the nibble appears insignificant.

Smart Tips & Tactics

■ **Plead lack of authority to grant the extras.** Say, "I simply don't have the authority to make the concessions. Departure from our standard conditions requires the explicit approval of our head office."

■ **Publish a price list that specifies the extra charges for all extras and details your firm's policies.** The written word always has more authority than the spoken word.

■ **Turn the nibbler's request down politely.** Most nibblers are only leading you on.

■ **Anticipate the nibble by including it in your original price.** Then allow the nibbler to think he has beaten you down.

StreetTalk

British soldier and explorer, and a favorite of Queen Elizabeth I, Sir Walter Raleigh was never backward in asking for royal favors and rewards. The Queen once rebuked him for his greed, "When will you cease to be a beggar?" "When you cease to be a benefactress, ma'am," replied Raleigh.

Add-On

The add-on tactic consists of adding on extras to the base terms of the deal.

Beware the Windscreen Price

Car sellers use the add-on tactic to dramatically boost their margins and profits. You look at the quoted price on the windscreen naively believing this is an all inclusive price. Then you discover the on-road price includes extras for the mag wheels, the performance tires and the high-performance sound system.

That's not all. The salesperson will then try to sell you more extras such as upholstery protectant and extended warranty.

Buying Tactics

Selling add-ons is a legitimate business tactic. Skilled buyers can use the same tactic only in reverse. "If you throw in extra service warranty, I'll buy this car" or, "If you install the computer free, we have a deal."

> You don't go broke making a profit.
>
> SIR NICHOLAS SHEHADIE
> AUSTRALIAN BUSINESS EXECUTIVE

Smart Tips & Tactics

■ **As a buyer never assume the initial price mentioned is the price you have to pay.** Sellers are trained to use the base price as bait.

■ **When buying ask,** "what's included in the price?" This makes the seller reveal the add-ons and limits their ability to invent additional "add-ons" once they think you've been hooked.

■ **Turn the add-on into a take-off.** Resist saying yes to the deal until the quoted price includes the add-ons you want.

■ **If you are a seller consider breaking your offer into component parts.** Set a basic price for the core and create add-on prices for the extras.

Street Talk

The Great Giveaway

Residuals are the extra payments actors receive after the initial airing or release of a film. Up until 1960, most actors got nothing for a film later shown on television. The winning of residual rights came after a bitter forty-two-day strike led by the Screen Actors Guild. The deal negotiated, by the then Screen Actors Guild president Ronald Reagan, has been called the Great Giveaway because Reagan gave away the residual rights for pre-1960 films for a paltry $2.6 million. Compare that to the $700 million actors currently receive annually for residuals.

Lack of Authority

No Authority
You negotiate a deal with someone you think has full authority to close the deal when the other side says, "I have to take this to my manager for approval."

It's remarkable how often this 'no authority' tactic leads to another round of negotiations and results in further concessions.

> Why should I question the monkey, when I can question the organ grinder?
>
> ANEURIN BEVAN
> BRITISH LABOR PARTY POLITICIAN

Monkeys and Organ Grinders
Union negotiators often claim they need to refer agreements to the membership "for final approval." It's remarkable how often Western businesspeople return from negotiations in countries such as Japan without ever knowing who are the "monkeys" and who are the "organ grinders."

Identify the Dominant Authority
Ask:
- Who spoke or acted with authority?
- Did one interrupt the others?
- Did one dominate the conversation?
- Who asked most of the questions?
- Who directly challenged our arguments most?

Smart Tips & Tactics

■ **Always ask the other party whether they have full authority to settle.** If you have any doubts add padding into your offer in anticipation of another round of concessions.

■ **Counter the no-authority tactic by qualifying your offer.** Say "I didn't appreciate our agreement needed further approval but that's okay. We treat this agreement as a statement of intent. While your manager checks it out, we'll also review for possible changes."

■ **Map the decision-making process.** Identify:
- Those who need to approve the deal.
- Those who have the power to veto the deal.

Street Talk

The Iranian Hostage Crisis

In 1980, during Jimmy Carter's presidency, the U.S. government spent ten months fruitlessly trying to negotiate the release of fifty-four Americans held hostage in Iran. The initial mistake: the U.S. government negotiated with the wrong people. They negotiated with Iran's secular leaders whereas the real power lay with Iran's religious leaders, in particular the Ayatollah Khomeni.

Take It or Leave It

That's My Final Offer

In most negotiations there comes a point when one side says, "That's my final offer." They might even aggressively add, "It's up to you, take it or leave it."

"Take it or leave it" used aggressively arouses great hostility. Nobody likes being threatened with an ultimatum.

Boulwarism

"Take it or leave it" offers don't have to be extreme. Some negotiators actually cultivate a reputation for not haggling. General Electric's vice president of relations service up to 1960, Lemuel R. Boulware, turned "take it or leave it" bargaining into an art form when negotiating with unions.

General Electric's offers were invariably fair. Nevertheless unions hated being disempowered. Boulwarism today is used to describe a negotiation tactic where one side decides what is fair and then makes a firm, final offer.

> Keep your friends close, but your enemies closer.
>
> AL PACINO (MICHAEL CORLEONE) IN THE MOVIE *THE GODFATHER, PART II*

Smart Tips & Tactics

■ **Test the "take it or leave it" by changing the nature of the package.** For example, "We could accept your final offer if you were prepared to deliver the fittings to our factory."

■ **Walk Out.** Call their bluff but leave the way open for the reopening of the talks without loss of face. For example, "We can't accept your final offer, I'm afraid we simply can't afford it. If however, you can find a way to reconsider your final offer, then please call me."

Street Talk

At the turn of the twentieth century, American Andrew Carnegie sold his steel interests for $300 million to fellow financial titan, J.P. Morgan. There were no negotiations. Carnegie hated haggling and liked to make his offers on a 'take it or leave it' basis. So he jotted his price onto a piece of paper which was handed to Morgan. Glancing at the paper, Morgan mumbled, "I accept." Years later, Carnegie ran into Morgan and said, "I should have asked for $500 million." "I would have paid it," replied Morgan.

120

Escalation

Changing the Game
Escalation is one of the most effective negotiation pressure tactics used. Sometimes it's ethical, sometimes it's not. It all depends upon the circumstances and the motives of the user.

Revising the Terms
You shop around for a 35-mm camera, set of lens and accessories, and eventually find a dealer who, after a lengthy bargaining session, offers to sell you the complete kit for $800.

You return the next day to pay for it when the seller says, "I'm sorry but the price we agreed to yesterday is too low. We simply can't afford to offer it to you at that price, the best we can do is $900."

What do you do? Walk away? Many people don't. They've invested too much time in the deal and it's too much trouble negotiating another deal with another company, so they agree to the "escalated price."

> If you are scared to go to the brink, you are lost.
>
> JOHN FOSTER DULLES
> FORMER U.S. SECRETARY OF STATE

Smart Tips & Tactics

■ **Call the other side's bluff.** This is the only effective way to deal with escalation. First, call for convincing evidence that the escalation is justified. If it isn't, walk away.

■ **Counter-escalate.** Be ready to respond with a counteroffer.

■ **Prepare for the worst if you use escalation tactics.** Negotiations can quickly degenerate into acrimony.

■ **Don't use escalation tactics if you later need to build trust.** Escalation tactics damage relationships.

Fighting Dirty

Nothing is more fatal than a dodge. Wrongs may be forgiven, sufferings and losses will be forgiven or forgotten . . . but anything like chicanery, anything like a trick, will always rankle.

WINSTON CHURCHILL
STATESMAN AND PRIME MINISTER OF BRITAIN

The Budget Limitation

This is All I Can Afford
Imagine you've just submitted a bid to redesign and renovate a client's premises for $268,000. Your client says, "I like your proposal, but I'm afraid all I've got is $155,000." Your client is using the budget limitation, or *bogey* tactic as it is sometimes called. You can either cut your price or come up with alternatives.

> I paid too much for it, but it's worth it.
>
> SAMUEL GOLDWYN
> FILM PRODUCER

The bogey price is entirely ethical. A legitimate budget limitation or bogey encourages the seller to cut her price and redesign her package to solve the buyer's budget problems.

Establishing Commitment
For budget limitation to have maximum impact the buyer first needs to convince the seller she really is committed to buying. Second, the buyer needs to convince the seller that the budget limitation is genuine and likely to hold for the foreseeable future.

Finally, the buyer needs to put the onus on the seller to come up with creative ways to bring their price down to the budget.

Smart Tips & Tactics

■ **To counter the budget limitation tactic prepare alternative packages in advance.** This puts the onus on the buyer to make the hard choices.

■ **Resell the value of your original package.** At the same time show the buyer what a cut in price will mean in terms of reduced quality and service.

■ **Consider changing the time frame for payments.** Extending payments into the next budget period can sometimes make your offer more affordable.

■ **Demand extra concessions in return for meeting the budget.** Consider asking for: a longer-term contract, additional services to be added to the base contract, or an increase in the minimum order size.

StreetTalk

The bogey (budget limitation tactic) should always be considered when purchasing a relatively complex product or service. Uncle Sam uses it when he gets a defense contractor to take a close look at his million-dollar proposal because the government budget is only $700,000. A school district uses it when it tells its architect to redesign the high-school building to fit the $2 million limitation imposed by the bond issue. An industrial buyer does it when he shows the salesman that the amount budgeted by the accounting department is less than what the seller bid.

CHESTER L. KARASS
FOUNDING DIRECTOR OF THE CENTER FOR EFFECTIVE NEGOTIATING[2]

Good Guy, Bad Guy

It's Always An Act
This act—and it is an act—is a variation of the good cop, bad cop interrogation routine.

The first interrogator—the bad cop—threatens to bully and bludgeon the prisoner into submission. The good cop adopts a much softer approach.

Commercial Variations
In commercial negotiations the tough guy adopts a competitive, uncompromising position. In a typical sales negotiation she declares, "We're not prepared to pay a cent above $2.80 a unit." The other negotiator adopts a softer stance. "Come on Carol, don't be unreasonable, Peter has always treated us well over the years. Surely we can go to $3.15."

If all goes to plan, the salesperson will grab the good guy's offer even though it is well below what is realistic.

> One should not be too straightforward. Go and see the forest. The straight ones are cut down, the crooked ones are left standing.
>
> KAUTILYA
> THIRD CENTURY B.C.
> INDIAN PHILOSOPHER

Smart Tips & Tactics

■ **The best defense is to recognize the tactic.**
The tough guy and the nice guy are a team—a duet.

■ **Call the tactic.** Openly describe what you believe the other party is doing.

■ **Go along with the ploy.** Then play the good cop off against the bad cop.

■ **Beware the "imaginary" behind the scenes bad cop.** He may not exist. So always ask to meet the other player.

A more subtle form of the (good guy, bad guy) tactic is to assign the "bad guy" the speaking role only when the negotiations are headed in a direction that the team does not want; as long as things are going well, the good guy does the talking.

Roy J. Lewicki, Joseph A. Litterer, John W. Minton, David M. Saunders, NEGOTIATION[3]

Outrageous Initial Demand

Russian Highball
When the Soviet Union opened their negotiations for the sale of the 1976 Olympic television rights with opening demand of $210 million, the U.S. networks howled in protest. They were expecting to pay around $75 million.

Revising Expectations
The Russians didn't get anywhere near their opening price but they did cause the American networks to revise their bids. Negotiators use ridiculously high (or low) opening offers to force the other side to re-evaluate their opening bid and expectations.

> A horse! A horse! My kingdom for a horse!
>
> Shakespeare's *Richard III*, Act V, Scene IV

Risks
Highball/lowball offers can work but they come with a huge risk. The other side may simply walk away because they think negotiating is a waste of time.

The Russians didn't face this danger over the Olympic rights negotiations, because they held a monopoly on television rights, plus the competing networks were collectively unlikely to walk away.

Smart Tips & Tactics

■ **Don't get rattled by the outrageous demand.**
It's invariably a bluff.

■ **Stick with your original offer.**
Carefully explain the basis for your offer, always reinforcing your credibility.

■ **Ask the other side for the rationale of their offer.** Then calmly demolish their case point by point.

■ **Accept that outrageous offers are part of highly competitive environments and cultures.** Here it pays to treat negotiations as if it were a sport.

Street Talk

Dealmaker Wayne Huizenga purchased hundreds of businesses while building Waste Management, Blockbuster Video and Republic Industries. When purchasing a business, Huizenga avoids lowball offers. Instead he opens with a reasonable offer within 5 to 10 percent of the final price he is willing to pay. Huizenga knows lowball offers insult business owners who have spent their lives building their businesses and with whom Huizenga wants an ongoing relationship.

Chicken

> It is much easier to apologize than to ask permission.
>
> Grace Murray Hopper
> Admiral

Commitment Tactics
Convincing the other side you have no freedom of choice can be a powerful tactic.

In the 1950s James Dean movie, *Rebel Without a Cause,* the characters play a game of chicken with cars. Two race headlong towards each other until one driver swerves at the last minute. The driver who swerves and loses his nerve is called "chicken."

Bluff Plus Threat
Negotiators who play chicken usually combine a big bluff with a threat to force the other side to 'chicken out' and concede what they want.

In an industrial dispute management may tell the union if they don't accept pay cuts they will close the plant. To stay credible, management has to follow through. So what should the union do? Management might be bluffing but what if management is telling the truth?

Smart Tips & Tactics

■ **Call the bluff.** In practice very few commitments are irreversible.

■ **Call the tactic.** If both sides play the game, throw away their steering wheels; both parties crash.

■ **Keep the negotiations private.** Commitments made in public or to the media are much more difficult to reverse.

Street Talk

Playing Chicken

In 1985, Frank Borman, the president of Eastern Airlines, threatened to sell the airline if he didn't get 20 percent wage cuts from all the airline's unions. One of the unions held firm and called his bluff, so Borman sold the Eastern Airline to the ruthless Frank Lorenzo. Lorenzo slashed wages and jobs and eventually destroyed the airline. Both sides played chicken but no one chickened out. Borman lost his beloved airline. The union members lost their jobs.

Reverse Auction

Intensifying the Competition
The reverse auction is one of the most fiercely competitive tactics used in negotiations. Let's say you have three bids or tenders for the installation of a new heating system. You intend to give the job to the lowest bidder, but when all the bids come in you find each one is a little different in terms, fittings and warranties.

Playing One Off Against the Others
You therefore invite all the bidders to your office and play one off against the others in a reverse auction.

You selectively quote from each of their bids, being careful to stress aspects where their rivals are better and where they need to improve.

The weaknesses in the three systems are also exposed as each of the rivals points out the weaknesses of the others. You finally give the job to the one offering the best package.

The reverse auction works because it intensifies the competitive process. That's why most sellers hate it.

> I've always realized that if I'm doing well at business, I'm cutting some other bastard's throat.
>
> KERRY PACKER
> AUSTRALIAN ENTREPRENEUR AND CHAIRMAN, CONSOLIDATED PRESS HOLDINGS

Smart Tips & Tactics

■ **If you are faced with an offer to rebid, decline it.** Reject it, on the grounds that it is unethical.

■ **If you have to rebid, make your bid last.** And then make only one bid.

■ **Don't rebid unless you are allowed to resell your package.** Support your presentation with credible experts.

■ **Set a bottom-line figure in advance and refuse to budge from it.** Remember the whole purpose of a reverse auction is to let the urge to beat your competitor overcome your need to make a profit.

■ **Use tough, battle-hardened negotiators.** The graveyard is full of inexperienced negotiators destroyed by reverse-auction tactics.

Street Talk

The reverse auction is not without its liabilities. Sellers who crack under pressure often get even later. They resent the auction and make up for the damage done them. Once the contract is gotten, they do not feel badly about charging a fat price for every design change. Many end up delivering late, shaving on quality and breaking promises.

CHESTER L. KARASS
FOUNDER OF THE CENTER FOR EFFECTIVE NEGOTIATING
AUTHOR, *GIVE & TAKE* [4]

Chapter Ten

PERSUASION TRAPS

How would you like a job where, if you made a mistake, a big red light goes on and 18,000 boo?

>	Jacques Plante
>	National Hockey League Goalie

Features
Virtually all negotiators fall into common psychological traps:

■ Learn to recognize and anticipate the twelve most common psychological traps.

■ Discover how you make critical decisions.

■ Learn how to use your head to manage your heart when under extreme emotional pressure.

Smart Negotiator, Dumb Deal

> I can calculate the motions of the heavenly bodies, but not the madness of people.
>
> Isaac Newton
> English scientist, astronomer and mathematician after losing his savings in the South Sea Bubble of 1720

Irrational Thinking

Human beings are not like Star Trek's Mr. Spock—strictly logical, focused on an end goal, free from mind-trapping emotions.

Congnitive psychologists have discovered we are not the logical, rational negotiators we like to think we are. We spend much of our lives with our minds locked unthinkingly on automatic pilot. As a result many of the decisions that go into a negotiation are made mindlessly with little or no thought at all.

Smart and Dumb Deals

A smart negotiation is one where we maximize our interests by negotiating rationally. A dumb negotiation is one where we knowingly negotiate a deal that is clearly not in our best interests.

Cognitive psychologists have identified the big mistakes we regularly make when we negotiate. In this section we identify twelve of the most costly errors. Fortunately, these blunders can be corrected.

Smart Tips & Tactics

■ **Learn to recognize the common psychological errors negotiators make.** Success starts with being able to identify potential blunders.

■ **Learn to understand the root causes of the key psychological mistakes.** To prevent mistakes you have to know what causes them.

■ **Audit the way you make decisions.** This will alert you to upcoming errors or traps.

■ **Audit your opponents' decision-making process.** Their distorted thinking can easily destroy a deal.

■ **Plan, plan, plan.** Good preparation helps you to distinguish good deals from bad and anticipate what might go wrong.

Street Talk

IBM's Dumbest Mistake?

When IBM produced the first PC in 1981, it immediately set the standard for what had been a fragmented market. But who made the super profits from the new standard. Not IBM. It was Microsoft that controlled and owned the operating standard. IBM's dumb mistake. It didn't bother to negotiate an ownership stake in Microsoft or its operating system. The cost of the mistake? Billions.

Trap 1: Over-Confidence, Ego, Hubris

Negotiators are persistently, and irrationally overconfident. Research shows dealmakers consistently overrate their talents, knowledge and skills.

Hubris
When overconfidence combines with arrogance or excessive pride the result is hubris.

Deals That Destroy Value
The best and most persuasive evidence of overconfidence and hubris comes from the world of corporate mergers and acquisitions. Empire-building CEOs have created what is now a three-trillion-dollar-a-year deal-making orgy.

Yet study after study—carried out over the last 30 years—shows two out of three mergers and takeovers fail. Instead of creating wealth for the buyer they destroy it. A prime reason: An overconfident buyer paid too much for the acquisition in the first place.

Overconfidence Persists
We stay overconfident because we habitually remember or inflate our successes but play down, repress or forget our failures.

> If I only had a little humility, I would be perfect.
>
> TED TURNER
> FOUNDER,
> TURNER BROADCASTING
> AND CNN

Smart Tips & Tactics

■ **Watch out for signs of overconfidence if you boast about your deal successes or explain away or gloss over your mistakes.** Top negotiators manage their egos by being honest about their mistakes.

■ **Keep a detailed summary of the results—all good and bad—of all your deals handy.** This is the best way to stop you forgetting about past errors.

■ **Add an "overconfidence discount" when you calculate your financial projections.** If forecasting the long-term profits from a deal—cut 25 percent from your most optimistic scenario. Then add 25 percent to your worst-case or downside scenario.

■ **Seek a second opinion.** Ask an expert to critique your decision-making processes.

Street Talk

Dumb Deal

In 1994 Quaker Oats purchased Snapple for $1.7 billion. Analysts at the time said that purchase price was as much as $1 billion too much. But the CEO confidently pushed ahead. "Snapple has tremendous growth potential through increased penetration, broader distribution and international expansion," he said. Twenty-eight months later Quaker off-loaded Snapple to Triac for $300 million, that is, for less than 20 percent of its original purchase price. The price of overconfidence: $1.4 billion.

Trap 2: Loss Aversion

Seek Pride and Avoid Regret
Psychologically we hate the pangs of regret that come from a loss and seek actions that cause pride. Regret is the pain that comes from a loss or bad decision. Pride is the joy that comes from a win or good decision.

> I hate to lose more than I like to win.
> — LARRY BIRD
> BASKETBALL STAR

Lock in Profits and Avoid Losses
Research shows when we buy stocks and they rapidly rise in price, we like to sell them quickly and lock in the profits. We can now boast about our talents to our friends. However, if some of the stock slumps in price we hold onto it and wait for the price to recover. As a result investors sell the stocks they should keep and keep the stocks they should sell.

Two researchers, Daniel Kahneman and Amos Tversky, found psychologically a loss has about *two and a half times* the impact of a gain of the same magnitude. Is it any wonder dealmakers cling to bad deals when they should cut their losses.

Smart Tips & Tactics

■ **Assess your tolerance for loss.** Review your past deals for tendencies to sell winning investments more readily than losing ones.

■ **Forget the past.** Don't be tempted to throw good money after bad by trying to salvage a poor past deal.

■ **Make sell decisions before you become emotionally tied.** For example, if you buy a product for investment decide in advance what price you will sell if the price declines.

■ **Commit to memory the futures' trader's adage "you have to love to take losses and hate to take gains."** This seemingly nonsensical saying reminds us to sell quickly and get out of a bad position when a market has turned sour.

Street Talk

Dumb Deal

In 1991 AT&T acquired NCR for $7.4 billion in a bid to become a major player in the computer business. Losses piled up. The deal quickly turned sour. But AT&T held on for five long years rather than cut its losses. When AT&T finally quit the investment it had lost $6.8 billion. The New York Times' *Floyd Norris* called the deal 'the worst merger of the century.' Incidentally as a result of the takeover AT&T sold its 19 percent stake in Sun Microsystems for some $700 million, realizing a profit of $183 million.

In August 2000, 19 percent of Sun was worth $35 billion. What if AT&T had held onto Sun—a proven winner and quit it loser—NCR?

Trap 3: Plunging In

First Impressions Count
We often plunge into poor deals because we don't take the time to systematically think through the reasons for them. An early rush of misplaced enthusiasm about a deal needn't be a problem, if you take the time to draw back and question your assumptions.

> Assumption is the mother of screw up.
>
> ANGELO DONGHIA
> DESIGNER

The Confirmation Trap
But instead of challenging our preconceptions we do the opposite. We look for reasons to confirm our first impressions, however misplaced.

Psychologists call this urge to reinforce our initial opinion the confirmation trap. We look for confirming evidence to support our initial thinking and in the process overlook or ignore disconfirming data.

The common saying "You don't get a second chance to make a first impression" is the result of the confirmation trap. Once people fix an idea in their head, they often hold onto it, however foolish it may be.

Smart Tips & Tactics

■ **Seek out second and third opinions when making key decisions.** This is the best way to avoid confirmation bias.

■ **Do your homework.** The more research you do the more likely you are to pay heed to disconfirming information.

■ **Be humble.** Admit you're not perfect and like everyone else make mistakes.

■ **Watch out for confirmation bias if you're especially loyal to brands.** Excessive brand loyalty is an extension of confirmation bias.

StreetTalk

Do you know that repeat buyers of Mercedes cars pay an average $7,410 more for a new car than buyers who switch to Mercedes from another brand. Mercedes owners want to confirm their decision to buy a Mercedes. Why? When Mercedes buyers shop for a second or third Mercedes they are looking for reasons to confirm that their previous decision to buy a Mercedes was the right one. As a result they don't bargain as hard as a buyer who is switching brands and considering Mercedes for the first time.

Trap 4: Anchoring

> It's not what you don't know that will hurt you. It's what you think you know that just ain't so.
>
> SATCHEL PAIGE
> BASEBALL PLAYER

Anchors Benchmark Us

A buyer offers you a much lower price than you think your property is worth. You think the offer borders on the ridiculous. Nevertheless you do accept the offer as a starting point, and in the end it does cause you to lower your expectations.

The buyers low opening offer acted as an **anchor** and became a benchmark against which you later judged the success of the whole deal.

Selling Real Estate

Anchors are widespread. Most homebuyers, for example, judge their success by the amount they can negotiate off the list price. The list price in effect becomes an anchor or reference point.

A smart negotiator would ignore the list price and instead commission an independent valuation to calculate what the house really is worth.

Pricing Diamonds

The trouble is most anchors work on us unconsciously. How much would you pay for an engagement ring? Most people reply "two months salary."

That's the anchor or benchmark that De Beers have not so subtly been promoting to us for years in endless 'diamonds are forever' advertisements.

Smart Tips & Tactics

■ **Multiply your anchors.** Anchoring poses its greatest risk when you allow a single fact or figure to benchmark you. So wherever possible use multiple anchors. When you value a property ask for an optimistic and pessimistic forecast. When you prepare a projected sales forecast, project a best-case and a worst-case scenario.

■ **Educate everyone on the dangers of anchoring.** Make sure everyone who works with you is aware of the perils of anchoring.

■ **Analyze each deal from different perspectives.** Exploring a deal from multiple perspectives will reduce the impact of anchoring.

The shape of the final deal is much more strongly influenced by initial offers than subsequent counter offers. "If an initial offer is too extreme, the negotiator must re-anchor the process, even if this means threatening to walk away from the table, rather than agreeing to an unacceptable starting point for the negotiation."

MAX BAZERMAN
J. JAY GERBER
DISTINGUISHED PROFESSOR OF DISPUTE RESOLUTION, KELLOGG GRADUATE SCHOOL, NORTHWESTERN UNIVERSITY[1]

Trap 5: Myopia

Shortsightedness
Myopia is shortsightedness. Negotiators suffer from myopia when they narrowly focus on the short-term aspects of a deal, ignoring the long term.

Chess grandmasters often plan eight to ten moves in advance. But, like amateur chess players, most negotiators only plan one or two moves ahead.

> It wasn't raining when Noah built the ark.
> HOWARD RUFF
> BUSINESS CONSULTANT

Ignoring the Future
Myopia causes negotiators to ignore or undervalue the long-term benefits or costs that might accrue from a deal.

The most common example of business myopia comes when businesses fail to anticipate how competitors will react to aggressive moves. A business cuts its prices without considering they might be triggering a price war.

Causes of Myopia
Why are we so myopic? Two reasons. One, we have to work harder to plan four or five steps ahead. Two, the short-term benefits and costs of a deal are much more vivid and real than the long-term ones, which are often uncertain and intangible.

Smart Tips & Traps

■ **Monitor your deals for myopic thinking.** Talking long-term and acting short-term is a common mistake.

■ **Use expert help to help you to consider your long-term options.** It often takes more than one head to consider alternative future scenarios.

■ **Don't let your initial reaction to short-term crises distort your long-term perspective.** Knee-jerk reactions often cause poor decisions.

Thinking Long-Term

A young girl visited a farm one day and wanted to buy a large watermelon.

"That's three dollars," said the farmer. "I've only got thirty cents," said the young girl.

The farmer pointed to a very small watermelon in the field and said, "How about that one?"

"Okay, I'll take it," said the little girl. "But leave it on the vine. I'll be back for it in a month."

Trap 6: Frame Blindness

> Seek simplicity, then distrust it.
>
> ALFRED NORTH WHITEHEAD
> ENGLISH MATHEMATICIAN AND PHILOSOPHER

Half Empty or Half Full

An optimist looks at a glass of water and views it as half full. The pessimist looks at the same glass and views it as half empty. In the same way, the way we view or frame information has a powerful effect on the way we negotiate.

Frames are mental structures that help us simplify and make sense of the confusing world in which we live. Frames control what information we pay attention to.

Framing a Deal

A dealmaker who frames a sale as a one-off transaction will adopt a difference tactic to a negotiator who frames a sale as part of a relationship. Research shows negatively framed negotiators give away fewer concessions and deadlock more than positively framed negotiators.

Most negotiators are unaware of their frames. A lifetime of training, experience and cultural stimuli condition us "to think like an accountant, an engineer or marketer."

Smart Tips & Tactics

- **Know your frame.** To analyze your frame ask:
  - What issues does our frame highlight?
  - What issues does our frame downplay or ignore?
  - What measure do we use to judge success?

- **Analyze their frame.** To discover another person's frame ask:
  - What do they talk about most?
  - What issues or facts do they downplay or ignore?
  - What measures will they use to judge success?

- **Align frames.** Try to blend your frame with the frame of the other party.

Persuading the Bishop

The young priest asks his bishop, "Will you give me permission to smoke while I pray?" The answer is an angry no. The older priest, also addicted, asks the same bishop, "May I have permission to pray while I am smoking?"

The answer: An enthusiastic yes. The way you frame a question can be the difference between a yes and no.

Trap 7: Focusing on Vivid Events

Jaws

When *Jaws*—the film starring a man-eating shark—opened at cinemas across the United States, the number of swimmers visiting California beaches dropped dramatically. Sharks do inhabit the California coast but the risk of a swimmer actually being attacked by a shark is very much less than the risk of being killed in a road accident while driving there.

Negotiators are often not influenced by the true facts of a situation. More often they are influenced by what makes the most vivid impression on their mind.

Vivid Information Distorts Thinking

Vivid information causes negotiators to misinterpret and distort evidence and end up making stupid decisions.

When it comes to calculating the probability of an event occurring, humans can be way off the mark. Ask someone what are the odds of a randomly selected jet flight on a major U.S. airline ending in a fatal crash? The actual odds are one in 10,000,000.

> The first rule of poker: If you look around the table and can't figure out who the sucker is, its you.
>
> GARY BELSKY AND THOMAS GILOVICH
> AUTHORS, *WHY SMART PEOPLE MAKE BIG MONEY MISTAKES*

Smart Tips and Tactics

■ **Check out the statistics whenever you make a critical forecast or estimate.** It's remarkable how often your "guesstimates" turn out to be wrong.

■ **Question your assumptions whenever you make an estimate or forecast.** Look for errors likely to be caused by vividness.

■ **Watch out for insurances or warranties that offer instant peace of mind.** If you can easily afford to incur the loss, you are probably better off carrying the risk.

■ **Whenever the other party uses a story or analogy to paint a vivid picture to persuade you, beware.** They're probably trying to scare you.

Street Talk

Dumb Deal

Insurance companies exploit vivid scares to sell us additional insurance policies and warranties.

Thirty percent of all new car buyers buy extended warranties. Forty percent of people shopping at electronics and appliance stores purchase extended warranties.

The seller of these insurance policies make super profits on these items. Why?

Because the odds of us ever claiming are very low. We would be far better off saving our insurance money and paying for the occasional breakdown.

Trap 8: Number Blindness

> Nothing defines human beings better than their willingness to do irrational things in the pursuit of phenomenally unlikely payoffs.
>
> Scott Adams
> creator of *Dilbert*

Ignorance Is Bliss

Virtually every Spaniard takes a ticket in the weekly National Lottery. One grand-prize winner was asked, "How did you do it? How did you know which ticket to buy?" He answered, "For seven nights in a row, I dreamed of number seven, since seven times seven is forty-eight . . ."

The winner clearly can't multiply. He doesn't even understand he is claiming credit for an event that was determined by random chance, something that was totally out of his control.

Innumeracy Is Widespread

But the fact remains, innumeracy (ignorance of mathematics) afflicts most negotiators.

Typically, negotiators miscalculate probabilities. They fall into the trap of ignoring the small numbers in deals, the cost of which can add up to a small fortune over time.

Smart Tips and Tactics

■ **Don't get carried away by short-term rewards.** It's what you earn or net in the long term that really counts.

■ **Cost the impact of inflation into every deal.** It can make a huge difference to your final returns.

■ **Beware of small numbers.** Pay particularly close attention to commission structures in investments and deals. Although nominally small, commission fees can add up to a small fortune over time.

■ **Beware of small samples.** Statistically they're highly unreliable and can lead to big mistakes.

■ **Don't look for patterns where none exist.** Events, such as a run of four sevens on a gaming table, are the results of random phenomena.

StreetTalk

The Extraordinary Power of Compounding

The Dutch bought Manhattan from the Indians in 1626—over 367 years ago—and they allegedly paid $24 for it. Were the Indians taken advantage of? If they had invested those $24 at 5 percent for 367 years—the investment would be worth $1.4 billion. That's assuming no taxes of course.

JAMES E STOWERS
AMERICAN BUSINESSMAN AND FOUNDER OF
TWENTIETH CENTURY MUTUAL FUNDS[2]

Trap 9: Irrational Commitment

Know When to Quit
Knowing when to quit or when to walk away from a deal separates the smart from the dumb dealmaker. Comedian W.C. Fields said it all: "If at first you don't succeed, try, try and try again. Then quit. No use being a damn fool about it."

Yet too often negotiators ignore Fields' advice. Committed to a course of action they become emotionally entrapped.

> A fanatic is one who can't change his mind and won't change the subject.
>
> WINSTON CHURCHILL
> STATESMAN AND PRIME MINISTER OF BRITAIN

Investment Fiascos
The history of investment fiascos provides dozens of examples. Investors buy stock when they think it is a bargain, and when it collapses they buy more of the same stock, since now it is an even better deal. The commitment and the dollars invested escalate out of control.

Fanaticism
What started out as a rational investment decision has turned into desperate folly? Fanaticism, says George Santayana, consists in redoubling your effort when you have forgotten your original aim.

Smart Tips and Tactics

■ **Know when to quit.** Irrational escalation is the result of misdirected persistence.

■ **Look out for disconfirming evidence.** The trick is to notice the warning signs of escalation before you get hooked.

■ **Stay away from price wars.** These and other high-risk plays can easily escalate out of control.

■ **Admit your mistakes early.** The embarrassment is small compared to the cost of titanic-size misadventures.

Street Talk

Dumb Deal

In 1987 Robert Campeau initiated a bidding war with Macy's for the control of Bloomingdales Department Stores. The bidding war became a contest of egos. On March 25, The Wall Street Journal declared "we're not dealing in price anymore but egos. What's being offered is top dollar, and beyond what anyone expected." On March 31, Macy's rejected a generous eleventh-hour offer from Campeau. So in revenge, Campeau topped Macy's offer by another $500 million. Bloomingdales was his. But at what cost. In January 1990, Campeau declared bankruptcy

Trap 10: Win-Lose Mindset

Hyper-Competitiveness
Hyper-competitive personalities often fall into the trap of treating negotiation as a contest. They can't bear to lose—or even share the spoils of a deal with another party. They win, you lose.

Fixed Pie Syndrome
The trouble is win-lose negotiators come to the deal table with the belief they are fighting for a slice of a fixed pie. Since they believe the size of the pie is fixed, negotiations become a battle over who gets the biggest slice.

Devaluation of Concessions
So, even when the other side offers generous concessions, the super-competitive personality automatically devalues the concessions—since they believe what is good for the other side has to be bad for them.

Single-Issue Price Negotiations
Win-lose negotiators also often reduce negotiations to one issue, usually money. As a result potentially good deals degenerate into acrimony.

> Let us be thankful for the fools. But for them the rest of us could not succeed.
>
> — Mark Twain
> Novelist and Humorist

Smart Tips and Tactics

■ **Multiply the issues.** Focusing on a single issue is the quickest way to turn a potentially cooperative deal into an adversarial one.

■ **Guard against reactive devaluation.** It's plain stupid to devalue or reject a concession simply because it comes from the other side.

■ **Expand the pie before you divide it.** Focus on how you can jointly expand the pie before you start splitting up the pie.

■ **Negotiate the process before you start bargaining.** The deal-making process can be as important as the content of a negotiation.

■ **Don't let positions drive out interests.** Discuss your interests or underlying concerns before taking a position on an issue.

Reactive Devaluation

"Reactive devaluation operates in many legal negotiations. Lawyers frequently report that clients who initially are enthusiastic to settle for a given amount are disappointed when the other side actually offers that amount. If a neutral or third party offered clients the same settlement they'd take it. But when it comes from the other side they back away."

ROBERT H. MNOOKIN, SCOTT R. PEPPERT, AND ANDREW S. TULUMELLO, AUTHORS, *BEYOND WINNING*[3]

Trap 11: The Lemming Effect

Lemmings are dumb creatures because when one panic-driven lemming charges over a cliff, other lemmings follow the first one blindly to their death.

Herd Behavior
In the same way dealmakers will pay higher and higher prices for property, paintings and companies simply because other people, whom for the most part they have never met, are willing to pay similar prices. Being one of the group or following the crowd is a powerful motivator.

> If you insist on going along with the herd you could well find yourself heading straight for the slaughterhouse.
>
> GARY BELSKY AND THOMAS GILOVICH
> AUTHORS, *WHY SMART PEOPLE MAKE BIG MONEY MISTAKES—AND HOW TO CORRECT THEM*

Wall Street calls this "investing with the herd." Financial advisers take advantage of you by preaching another Wall Street aphorism: "The trend is your friend." Translated this says, "don't think"—follow the herd. Smart dealmakers should know better.

It's Safe to Conform
Skillful sellers take advantage of our psychological need to conform. A million dollar investment in a new computer system seems far less risky if you know others who have made the same choice.

Smart Tips and Tactics

■ **Be suspicious of anything called "hot."** Hot deals have a habit of rapidly turning "cold."

■ **Be patient and take the time to research every large deal.** Resist all temptations to consummate a quick deal.

■ **Focus on the long term.** Be wary of deals that are based on getting in early and cashing out quickly. These are notoriously risky.

■ **Be a contrarian.** Trend followers usually pay a premium for jumping into bandwagons. Do the opposite; look for currently unpopular opportunities that have good long-term potential.

Street Talk

You may be prone to following the herd if:

You invest in "hot" stocks or other popular investments.

You make spending and investment decisions based solely on the opinions of friends, colleagues, or financial advisers.

Your spending decisions are heavily influenced by which products, restaurants, or vacation spots are "in."

GARY BELSKY AND THOMAS GILOVICH, AUTHORS, *WHY SMART PEOPLE MAKE BIG MONEY MISTAKES—AND HOW TO CORRECT THEM*[4]

Trap 12: The Winner's Curse

Paying Too Much
In 1990 Ryoei Sato, the chairman of a Japanese paper firm, paid nearly $83 million for van Gogh's *Portrait of Dr. Cachet* at an international art auction. Most professional buyers, observing from the sidelines, said Sato had overpaid. The $83 million was twice the expected price. Sato had fallen victim to what psychologists call the winner's curse.

If you've ever been part of a competitive negotiation process where you kept upping the price until the last competitor dropped out, you've probably experienced the winner's curse. The curse comes when you discover you've paid far too much for your acquisition.

The Damage
The damage caused by the winner's curse can be huge. A BusinessWeek analysis of 302 major mergers carried out between 1995 and 2001, shows 61 percent of buyers destroyed shareholder wealth by overpaying.

> I don't want to belong to any club that will accept me as a member.
>
> GROUCHO MARX
> COMEDIAN AND FILM ACTOR

Smart Tips and Tactics

■ **Set an upper price limit and stick to it.** The best deals are sometimes the deals you walk away from.

■ **Add a margin of safety into your price.** The difference between the price you pay and the value you get is the safety margin.

■ **Be especially cautious where there are lots of competitors and great uncertainty over the price.** The winner's curse thrives in these conditions.

■ **Inoculate yourself against over commitment.** Role-play walking away from the deal and announcing to the press your reasons for quitting negotiations.

America Online's $50 Billion Write-off

The merger deal frenzy of the late 1990s included the biggest ever merger: America Online's $166 billion, all-stock bid for Time Warner in January 2000. The cost? In April 2002 AOL declared a $54 billion write-off to account for the subsequent fall in value.

Chapter Eleven

ELECTRONIC BARGAINING

Your medium or mode of communication is in and of itself a negotiating tactic.
　　Robert Mayer
　　American Attorney and Dealmaker

Features
Electronic bargaining is full of perils.

- Learn how to bargain on the telephone.
- Master the process of negotiating by e-mail.

Bargaining on the Telephone

Phone Power
The telephone can be a potent negotiation weapon. Research shows that telephone negotiations typically result in lots of one-sided deals. The party that knows how to exploit the phone can gain a real edge.

Fundamental Errors
The losing side in a telephone negotiation typically makes two fundamental errors:

■ They let the other party initiate and control the conversation. It's extraordinarily easy to make concessions or disclose valuable information when you're caught on the phone unprepared. Caught unprepared, negotiators make vague, ambiguous comments which often cause later problems.

■ They don't appreciate the value of deep listening. Skilled phone users rarely interrupt. They listen hard, searching for mismatches between the words said and tone of voice. It is actually easier to detect deception on the phone than it is in face-to-face conversation.

> If the phone doesn't ring it's me.
> TITLE OF SONG RECORDED BY JIMMY BUFFETT

Smart Tips & Tactics

■ **Pick your time and wherever possible initiate the phone call.** If you're unprepared, don't negotiate.

■ **Write down what you want to say, as well as what you don't want to say, before you make the call.** Negotiators commonly give away too much information when on the phone.

■ **Make an extra effort to speak clearly.** Telephone negotiations are characterized by increased misunderstandings and misinterpretations.

■ **Don't interrupt.** Interruptions irritate and lesson your chances of picking up valuable clues from the other party's tone of voice.

■ **Use silence to increase information disclosures.** Lots of negotiators feel compelled to fill conversation voids with helpful discourses.

StreetTalk

To confirm that you've been getting through, conclude the telephone conversation by reviewing the points that were agreed to. Your follow-up letter will reinforce the other person's telephone commitments.

ROBERT MAYER
ATTORNEY AND DEALMAKER[1]

Negotiating by E-Mail

People Negotiate Differently by E-Mail
When negotiators shift from face-to-face to e-mail negotiations they change their behavior.

A recent Harvard Business School study compared the impact of e-mail, telephone and face-to-face negotiations. Researchers found when people negotiate face to face they reach agreement some 80 percent of the time. When people negotiate by phone the most likely result is one that heavily favors one side. When people negotiate by e-mail the most common result is deadlock. Over 50 percent of e-mail negotiations end in impasse.

> I really didn't say everything I said.
> YOGI BERRA
> BASEBALL PLAYER AND MANAGER

Advantages of E-Mail
The big advantage of e-mail is the speed and cost of savings. You can also communicate in your own time away from the pressures that are associated with face-to-face negotiations.

Disadvantages of E-Mail
Unfortunately, when we negotiate by e-mail we become more abrupt, competitive and casual. The total absence of "body talk" results in more clashes, longer decision times and more extreme decisions.

Smart Tips & Tactics

■ **Always consider alternative communication channels.** Ask whether e-mail is the best way to resolve this issue?

■ **Soften your language.** Above all, guard against abruptness.

■ **Increase the social chat.** Spend time up front sharing social information.

■ **Don't rush to closure.** Take extra time to check out assumptions and deal with emotional needs.

■ **Use short words, short sentences and short paragraphs.** Long, jargon-laden e-mails cause angst and encourage the other side to read between the lines.

Schmoozing

It pays to go out of your way to establish both similarity and interpersonal liking when you must solve a negotiating problem with someone online. Even explicit schmoozing that might feel somewhat artificial given the informality of e-mail will probably help smooth the path toward agreement.

G. RICHARD SHELL, AUTHOR
ELECTRONIC BARGAINING[2]

Chapter Twelve

PLAN FOR SUCCESS

Plan your work and work your plan.
   ANONYMOUS

Features
Planning in negotiation is a key to success.

- Use the Mills One-Page Planner to scope your deals.
- Never negotiate without planning.

How to Plan a Negotiation

1. **Identify Your Interests**
   For each position
   Ask: Why do I really want this?

2. **Identify, Rank and Value Your Issues**
   a. List the issues
      Ask: What precisely do we need to achieve our interests?
   b. Rank your issues
      - High priority
      - Medium priority
      - Low priority
   c. Value each issue
      - Price each issue within a specific range

3. **Determine Your BATNA**
   Ask: What could we do if we don't reach agreement?

4. **Identify Your Counterpart's:**
   - Interests
   - Issues (list, rank and value)
   - BATNA

5. **Identify Potential Trade-Offs**
   Ask: What can we trade that is cheap for us and valuable for them?

6. **Compare BATNAs**
   Ask: Who has the stronger BATNA?

7. **Identify Information Gaps**
   On a separate page list what you don't know about your counterpart's intentions.

8. **Plan Your Strategy and Tactics**
   Consider:
   - The relationship
   - The balance of power
   - The degree of trust

The Mills One-Page Planner

One-Page Planner	
Our Interests	**Their Interests**
Our Issues	**Their Issues**
High Priority	*High Priority*
Medium Priority	*Medium Priority*
Low Priority	*Low Priority*
Our BATNA	**Their BATNA**

© Harry Mills 2005

Appendix A

ASSESS YOUR BARGAINING STYLE

Personal Bargaining Style

How do you react to conflict? Psychologists have identified five basic negotiation personality styles focused on how we handle interpersonal conflict.

Take the *Personal Bargaining Style Assessment* to diagnose your preferred bargaining style.

This assessment allows you to identify your typical bargaining style.

Read each of the statements below. Each one describes a negotiating behavior. Circle a number between 1 and 5. The numbers range from 1—does not describe me at all, to 5—describes me very well.

Description
1. I'm happy to bluff, exaggerate or play games in a negotiation if I believe I can get away with it.   1   2   3   4   5
2. I like to encourage the other side to be open by showing my willingness to share information.   1   2   3   4   5
3. I prefer to compromise rather than engage in long negotiations.   1   2   3   4   5
4. I give away more than I should to avoid conflicts.   1   2   3   4   5
5. I stay away from people who have issues that they need to resolve with me.   1   2   3   4   5

6. I try to reveal as little as possible about my needs when I negotiate.   1 2 3 4 5
7. I exchange information and ideas openly and honestly.   1 2 3 4 5
8. I don't like using ploys or gambits when a simple compromise would solve the problems.   1 2 3 4 5
9. People say I don't stick up for myself when I should.   1 2 3 4 5
10. I prefer to avoid controversy with my complaints or concerns.   1 2 3 4 5
11. I am happy to agree strongly if it means I can get my way.   1 2 3 4 5
12. I always try to uncover common interests whenever I negotiate.   1 2 3 4 5
13. I always look for opportunities to split the difference.   1 2 3 4 5
14. I try to help the other party even if it means making sacrifices.   1 2 3 4 5
15. Unless the rewards for negotiation are substantial, I will happily avoid it.   1 2 3 4 5
16. I am happy to use whatever leverage I have to meet my needs.   1 2 3 4 5
17. I try to be creative and come up with fresh ways to solve problems.   1 2 3 4 5
18. I often propose a middle way that works for both parties.   1 2 3 4 5
19. Building and maintaining a good relationship is important to me.   1 2 3 4 5
20. If I can ever avoid a negotiation I will.   1 2 3 4 5
21. I strongly compete for every concession I can win.   1 2 3 4 5
22. I like to turn conflicts into problem solving sessions.   1 2 3 4 5
23. I like to split the difference if the other side is prepared to move.   1 2 3 4 5

24. I rarely feel I can get what I want by negotiating.   1   2   3   4   5
25. I try to stay away from conflict wherever possible.   1   2   3   4   5

Scoring Key for Your Bargaining Style

Transfer the number you have circled to the corresponding spaces in the scoring key. Do this for all twenty-five questions. Then add up your total score for each of the five columns.

1.		2.		3.		4.		5.	
6.		7.		8.		9.		10.	
11.		12.		13.		14.		15.	
16.		17.		18.		19.		20.	
21.		22.		23.		24.		25.	
	Competing		**Collaborating**		**Compromising**		**Accommodating**		**Avoiding**

The column with the biggest total represents your natural negotiating style. The second highest total represents your next preferred style. The column with the lowest score is your least-preferred style.

The Five Basic Bargaining Styles

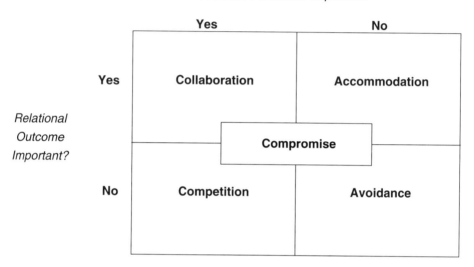

Avoiding Style

Conflict Avoiders strongly dislike the interpersonal conflict that often characterizes negotiation. They believe conflict is unproductive, prefer peace and quiet and actively avoid situations that expose them to conflict and disagreement.

Competing Style

Competitors thrive on the cut and thrust of conflict. Above all they love to win. The most aggressive view life as a contest where there are winners and losers.

Collaborating Style

Collaborators are problem solvers who look for win-win agreements that satisfy both sides.

Accommodating Style

Accommodators resolve problems by solving the other side's problems. Accommodators are even prepared to give in on substantive issues in order to preserve the relationship. They prize strong relationships and love to be liked.

Compromising Style
Compromisers strongly believe in fairness and like to maintain good working relationships with others. Compromisers are usually prepared to split the difference rather than haggle to the bitter end.

Managing the Clash of Styles
Having an awareness of your dominant bargaining styles means you can:
- Predict how you will react to different types of conflict situations.
- Diagnose others' conflict tendencies.
- Understand how different styles interact.

Appendix B

CHECKLIST OF BODY LANGUAGE GESTURES

One of the biggest mistakes you can make in observing body language is to make judgments on the basis of a solitary gesture. Gestures come in clusters and should always be interpreted this way.

Openness
- Warm smile
- Unfolded arms
- Uncrossed legs
- Leaning forward
- Relaxed body
- Direct eye contact with dilated pupils
- Open palms
- Unbuttoned/removed coat (for men)
- Hand/s to chest (for men)

Defensiveness
- Little eye contact
- Corners of lips turned down
- Rigid body
- Clenched hands
- Palm to back of neck
- Tightly crossed arms
- Wrinkled brow
- Tight pursed lips
- Head down
- Tightly crossed legs/ankles
- Scratching below ear lobes or side of neck

Dominance
- Palms down
- Straddling a chair—sitting with the chair back serving as a shield
- Feet on desk
- Physical elevation above the other person
- Stride, loud voice
- Leaning back in chair with both hands supporting head
- Strong palm-down thrusting or knuckle-crunching handshake
- Leg over arm of chair
- Using desk as a physical barrier

Aggressiveness
- Furrowed brow
- Sustained eye contact with contracted pupils (stare)
- Pointing glasses
- Clenched fist/s
- Squinting of the eyes
- Downward-turned eyebrows
- Pointed index finger
- Strong palm-down thrusting or knuckle-crunching handshake

- Arms spread out while hands grip the edge of table
- Leg over arm of chair

Boredom or Indifference
- Blank stare
- Lack of eye blinking
- Head in palm of hand
- Repetitive finger or foot tapping

Frustration
- Staring into space
- Running fingers through hair
- Kicking at ground or an imaginary object
- Short in-and-out breaths
- Wringing of hands

Readiness
- Good eye contact
- Seated, leaning forward with hands on mid thigh or knees
- Lively facial expression
- Standing with coat open and pushed back with hands on hips (for men)

Confidence
- Steepling of hands (joining fingers like a church steeple)
- Feet on desk
- Leaning back with hands joined behind back of head
- Proud erect stance with hands joined behind back

Nervousness, Uncertainty
- Weak, clammy handshake
- Constant throat clearing
- Hands covering mouth while speaking
- Poor eye contact
- Nervous laughter
- Tapping fingers on table

- Hands-on-hips when standing
- Moving in on the other person's personal territory

- Little eye contact
- Drooping eyes
- Crossed legs
- Doodling

- Tightly closed lips
- Rubbing back of neck
- Taking deep breaths
- Tightly clenched hands
- Pacing

- Alert facial expression
- Close proximity
- Sitting on edge of chair
- Nodding in agreement

- Head up
- Stretched legs
- Physically elevating oneself
- Leaning back in chair
- Continuous eye contact
- Chin forward

- Sighing
- Crossed arms and legs
- Fidgeting in chair
- Fiddling with objects, clothing
- Pacing
- Smoking
- Biting or picking fingernails or cuticles

Appendix C

CHECKPOINTS: STEPS 1 TO 7—THE RESPECT MODEL

Step 1: Ready Yourself

Checkpoints:
- Develop a BATNA
- Identify your interests
- Identify your opponent's interests
- List, rank and value the issues
- Gather information
- Analyze the other party
- Role play the negotiation beforehand
- Test your assumptions
- Consult with others
- Determine the limits of your authority
- Plan your agenda
- Determine your first offer
- Choose your team members
- Devise a time plan
- Choose a venue
- Assess your appetite for risk
- Manage your risks
- Strive for fairness
- Look out for signs of deceit
- Guard your reputation
- Plan your strategy
- Choose appropriate tactics

Step 2: Explore Needs

Checkpoints:
- Establish your credibility
- Communicate your opening position
- Influence with questions
- Avoid destructive questions
- Reflect the content of the other side
- Reflect the other side's feelings
- Listen for signals and clues
- Regularly summarize where you are at
- Create a positive, open non-verbal climate
- Speak clearly and confidently
- Use assertive persuasive language
- Use words that sell
- Use silence for effect
- Translate all meta-talk

Step 3: Signal for Movement

Checkpoints:
- Listen intently for signals showing movement
- Clarify all signals with follow-up questions
- Reciprocate with your own signals
- Repeat or reword missed signals

Step 4: Probe with Proposals

Checkpoints:
- Probe to elicit information
- Use proposals to clarify priorities
- Propose, then go quiet
- State your condition first and be specific
- Use the if/then technique
- Never interrupt a proposal
- Don't instantly reject a proposal
- Avoid the proposed killer "I disagree"
- Don't immediately counter with your own proposal
- Give as detailed a response as possible
- Indicate areas of agreement
- Regularly summarize where you are at
- Repackage proposals to make them more acceptable
- Multiply the variables to create more options and win-win packages

Step 5: Exchange Concessions

Checkpoints:
- Link issues, don't trade piecemeal
- Give yourself plenty of room to negotiate
- If you're selling, start high
- If you're buying, start low
- All offers should be realistic and credible
- Control and monitor your concession rate
- Avoid making the first major concession
- Trade reluctantly
- Concede slowly
- Conserve concessions for last minute trades
- Preface all offers with a condition
- Justify all concessions
- Track all concessions—yours and theirs
- Build momentum by emphasizing common interests
- Reward, don't punish, concessions
- Don't turn minor issues into matters of principle

- Start with small concessions
- Make sure the other side reciprocates
- Shift issues at impasses
- Handle ridiculous offers with care

Step 6: Close the Deal

Checkpoints:
- Decide at what point you want to stop trading
- Assess whether it is the right time
- Look out for body language cues
- Listen for questions that indicate a readiness to close
- Test the waters with a trial close
- Start with a summary close
- If necessary consider other possible closes
- Guard against deadline pressures
- Use body language to project a confident image
- Try to anticipate and avoid last minute deadlocks
- Consider changing the negotiator or using a mediator
- Keep questioning and listening

Step 7: Tie Up the Loose Ends

Checkpoints:
- Verify what has been agreed to
- Put the agreement in writing
- Volunteer to do the writing
- Write the agreement in plain explicit language
- Question every ambiguity
- Write up the agreement before separating
- Plan for future differences
- Review your performance

Appendix D

RECOMMENDATIONS FOR FURTHER READING

If you still have an appetite to read more on negotiation, I recommend the following titles.

Babcock, Linda and Sarah Laschever. *Women Don't Ask: Women and the Gender Divide,* Princeton University Press, 2003.
Babcock and Laschever show why women don't ask for what they deserve in negotiations. It shows women how to ask and why they should. Essential reading for both men and women.

Cohen, Herb. *You Can Negotiate Anything.* Angus and Robertson, London, 1982; Lyle Stuart, Secaucus, New Jersey, 1980.
The most readable, racy guide on negotiation there is, with lots of amusing anecdotes. Cohen knows how to negotiate, is street smart, and shows it. Unfortunately the book concentrates on strategies, tactics and ploys to the virtual exclusion of everything else.

Fisher, Roger and William Ury. *Getting to Yes.* Century Hutchinson, London, 1983; Houghton Mifflin, Boston, 1981.
The best introduction to joint problem-solving available. Some of Fisher and Ury's guiding principles—focus on interests not positions, develop a BATNA, invent options for mutual gain—should be drilled into every trainee negotiator. An essential read and highly readable too.

Fisher, Roger and Scott Brown. *Getting Together.* Century Hutchinson, London; Houghton Mifflin, Boston, 1988.
The sequel to *Getting to Yes, Getting Together* shows how to build long-term relationships that really work. Full of common sense that, unfortunately, is not so common.

Kennedy, Gavin. *Everything is Negotiable.* Arrow Books, London; Prentice Hall, Englewood Cliffs, New Jersey 1999.
A highly readable examination of the common problems negotiators face and how to handle them. The book is illustrated with scores of examples drawn from the world of international business. Anything Gavin Kennedy writes on negotiation is worth reading.

Kennedy, Gavin. *Pocket Negotiator.* Basil Blackwell, Oxford and The Economist Publications, London; Basil Blackwell, New York, 1987.
Organized like a dictionary, every serious negotiator should own a copy of this invaluable desk guide.

Kolb, Deborah M. and Judith Williams. *The Shadow Negotiation, How Women Can Master the Hidden Agenda That Determines Bargaining Success,* Simon & Schuster, 2000.
The Shadow Negotiation shows women a whole new way to think about the negotiation process and turn their strengths to their advantage. This valuable guide is a must read.

Lax, David A. and James K. Sebenius. *The Manager as Negotiator: Bargaining for co-operation and competitive gain.* Free Press Inc., New York; Collier Macmillan, London, 1987.
This is the definitive guide on how managers negotiate. Used as a text in many business school courses, this book is one of the few that deserves to be read two or three times.

Deiner, Marc. *Deal Power: 6 Foolproof Steps to Making Deals of Any Size.* Henry Holt, New York, 1997.
A highly practical handbook written by a knowledgeable, street-smart entertainment and business attorney. Remarkably easy to read and full of incisive quotations.

Mnookin, Robert H., Scott R. Peppet, and Andrew Tulumeillo. *Beyond Winning: Negotiating to Create Value in Deals and Disputes.* The Belknap Press of Harvard University Press, Cambridge, Massachusetts, 2000.
Beyond Winning is the best book on negotiation specifically aimed at lawyers. However all negotiators should read this cutting-edge book.

Raiffa, Howard with John Richardson, and David Metclakfe. *Negotiation Analysis: The Science and Art of Collaborative Decision Making.* The Belknap Press of Harvard University Press, Cambridge, Massachusetts, 2002.
If you want to know the research and analytical thinking that underpins the latest thinking on negotiation, read this book. Howard Raiffa is the author of several classic books on negotiation.

Shell, G. Richard. *Bargaining for Advantage: Negotiation Strategies for Reasonable People.* Penguin Group, New York, USA, 1999.
G. Richard Shell is director of the highly acclaimed Wharton Negotiation Workshop. Shell's framework and advice is practical, insightful and easy to read.

Stiebel, Dr. David. *When Talking Makes Things Worse! Resolving Problems When Communication Fails,* Whitehall & Nolton, 1997.
This book is one of the few practical negotiation books to show you what to do when understanding is not enough. Stiebel's four-step strategic communication model stems from his work as a negotiation adviser to corporate and government leaders.

Ury, William. *Getting Past No: Negotiating with Difficult People,* Bantam Books, 1991.
William Ury is co-author of the million-copy bestseller *Getting to Yes.* In *Getting Past No,* William Ury shows you how to get to yes when the other people say no. Ury's five-step strategy works and is easy to grasp.

NOTES

Chapter One
[1] Michael Watkins, *Breakthrough Business Negotiation,* Jossey Bass, 2002, p. 77.
[2] Leigh Thompson, *The Mind and Heart of the Negotiator,* 2nd edition, Prentice Hall, 2001, p. 5.
[3] Howard Raiffa, John Richardson and David Metcalfe, *Negotiation Analysis,* The Belknap Press of Harvard University Press, 2002, p. 114.

Chapter Two
[1] James C. Freund, *Smart Negotiating,* Simon & Schuster, 1992, p. 46.
[2] Kare Anderson, *Getting What You Want,* Dutton (Penguin), 1993, p. 64.
[3] Chester L. Karrass, *Give and Take,* Thomas Y. Crowell, 1974, pp. 18–22.
[4] Gavin Kennedy, *Pocket Negotiator,* The Economist Publications, 1987, p. 12.
[5] Alan N. Schoonmaker, *Negotiate to Win,* Prentice Hall, 1989, p. 65.
[6] Kennedy, *Pocket Negotiator,* pp. 234–235.
[7] Forbes Global, *Fuel's Paradise,* Forbes Global, January 20, 2003, p. 32.

Chapter Three
[1] Marc Diener, *Deal Power,* Henry Holt, 1997, p. 127.
[2] Harry Mills, *Artful Persuasion,* AMACOM, 1999, p. 44.
[3] Diener, *Deal Power,* p. 51.
[4] Leonard Koren and Peter Goodman, *The Haggler's Handbook,* Norton, 1993, p. 33.
[5] Bob Woolf, *Frendly Persuasion,* G. P. Putnam, 1990, p. 110.
[6] Robert Mayer, *Power Play,* Random House, 1996, p. 45.

Chapter Four
[1] Gavin Kennedy, *The New Negotiating Edge,* Nicholas Brearley, 1998, p. 157.

Notes

Chapter Five
[1] Kare Anderson, *Getting What You Want,* Dutton (Penguin), 1993, p. 147.
[2] Eric Wm. Skopec and Laree S. Kiely, *Everything's Negotiable,* AMACOM, 1998, p. 48.

Chapter Six
[1] Leo Hindery, Jr., *The Biggest Game of All,* Free Press, 2003, p. 64.
[2] G. Richard Shell, *Bargaining for Advantage,* Viking, 1999, p. 165.
[3] Linda Babcock and Sara Lascheves, *Women Don't Ask: Negotiation and the Gender Divide,* Princeton University Press, 2003.
[4] Leigh Thompson, *The Mind and Heart of the Negotiator,* Prentice Hall, 2001, p. 65.

Chapter Seven
[1] Brian Muldoon, *The Heart of Conflict,* Pedigree, 1996, p. 93.
[2] Leo Hindery, Jr., *The Biggest Game of All,* Free Press, 2003, p. 61.
[3] William Ury, *Getting Past No,* Bantam, 1991, pp. 40–44.
[4] Max Bazerman, James J. Gillespie, "Betting on the Future: The Virtues of Contingent Contracts," *Harvard Business Review,* Sept–Oct, 1999, pp. 155–160.

Chapter Nine
[1] Steven Click, Rachel Croson, "Reputation in Negotiations," *Wharton on Making Decisions,* ed., Hock, Kunreuther and Gunther, John Wiley, 2001, p. 178.
[2] Chester L. Karass, *Give & Take,* Thomas Y. Crowell, 1974, pp. 18–22.
[3] Roy J. Lewicki, Joseph A. Litterer, John W. Minton, David M. Saunders, *Negotiation,* Irwin, 1994, p. 74.
[4] Karass, *Give & Take,* p. 180.

Chapter Ten
[1] Max H. Bazerman, *Smart Money Decisions,* John Wiley, 1999, p. 22.
[2] James E. Stower, *Yes You Can . . . Achieve Financial Independence,* Andrews and McPhail, 1994, p. 27.
[3] Robert H. Mnookin, Scott R. Peppert and Andrew S. Tulumello, *Beyond Winning: Negotiating to Create Value in Deals and Disputes,* Belknapp Press, 2000, p. 166.
[4] Ibid.

Chapter Eleven

[1] Robert Mayer, *Power Plays,* Random House, 1996, p. 36.
[2] G. Richard Shell, "Electronic Bargaining: The Perils of Email and The Promise of Computer Assisted Negotiations," *Wharton on Making Decisions,* Eds., Stephen J. Hock, Howard C. Kunreuther with Robert E. Gunther, p. 209.

INDEX

accommodators, 174–175
acquisitions, impact of overpaying, 158
Adams, Scott, 150
add-on tactics, 114–115
agenda
  negotiating, 18, 19
  planning, 18
aggressive language, 56
aggressiveness, gestures indicative of, 177
agreements
  checkpoints, 183
  contingent contracts, 100–101
  enforceability of, 104
  and memo of understanding, 105
  plain language used for, 105
  verification of, 104
analyst, role of, 25
anchors, 142–143
Anderson, Kare, 15, 71
assertive language, 23, 56
AT&T, 139
authority
  being sure of, 20
  identification of, 116
  no-authority tactic, 117
  setting limits of, 20

Babcock, Linda, 82, 83
bargaining
  by e-mail, 164–165
  by telephone, 162–163
bargaining range, 8
  avoiding early disclosure, 48

negative zones, 9
bargaining styles
  described, 174–175
  management of, 175
  self-assessment, 171–173
BATNA
  defined, 12
  identifying opponent's, 29
  revealing one's, 13
  stages of, 12
Bazerman, Max, 101, 143
Belsky, Gary, 148, 156
Berra, Yogi, 40, 164
Best Alternative To a Negotiated Agreement, see BATNA
Bevan, Aneurin, 116
Bierce, Ambrose, 78
Bird, Larry, 138
body language
  checklist, 176–179
  as clues for closure, 94, 95
  impact of, 50
  proper posture tips, 51
bogey tactic, 122
Boon, Louise E., 30
Borman, Frank, 129
Boulware, Lemuel R., 118
boulwarism, 118
budget limitation tactic, 122–123
Buffett, Jimmy, 162

Campeau, Robert, 153
Carnegie, Andrew, 119
Carter, Jimmy, 117
Case, Steve, 98

Index

"chicken" tactic, 128–129
Churchill, Winston, 72, 121, 152
claims
  avoiding exaggerations, 47
  need for written record, 39
  verification of, 39
Click, Steven, 111
closing the deal
  checking for gestures, 95
  checkpoints for, 182–183
  listening for clues, 94
  splitting the difference, 98–99
  summary close, the, 96
  timing, 94
  weighing the close, 98–99
Cohen, Herb, 17, 27, 69
collaborators, 174
commitment
  irrational, 152–153
  tactics, 128–129
competitors, 174
compounding, 151
compromisers, 175
concessions
  avoiding the first move, 84
  avoiding tit-for-tat, 85
  checkpoints for, 181
  and competitive personalities, 154
  conditional, 77
  cost of, 76
  guarding against rejection of, 155
  to meet bogey tactic, 123
  strategies for, 84
  as tactic, 81, 85
  tracking of, 77
  trading of, 76
confidence, gestures indicative of, 178
confirmation trap, 140–141
conflict avoiders, 174
contingent contracts
  defined, 100
  need for clear terminology, 101
  purpose of, 101
contracts, see agreements
Coolidge, Calvin, 60
cooperation, through questions, 53

counter-offers, 79
creativity, in packaging proposals, 72
credibility
  expertise as key to, 46
  formula for, 46
  use of supporting evidence, 47
  value of endorsements, 47
Croson, Rachel, 111

deadlines
  avoiding disclosure of, 26
  creating momentum with, 27
  dealing with pressure of, 92
  exploiting differences in, 86
  identifying opponent's, 29
deadlocks, avoidance of, 93
deceit
  clues to, 41
  as common practice, 38
  detection of , see lie detection
  guarding against, 39
defensiveness, gestures indicative of, 176–177
Diener, Marc, 49, 53
differences, acknowledgment of, 97
dominance, gestures indicative of, 177
Donghia, Angelo, 140
Duke, James B., 79
Dulles, John Foster, 120

Edison, Thomas, 61
Eisenhower, Dwight D., 18
Ekman, Paul, 40
e-mail, negotiating by, 164–165
empathy, creation of, 54
Epictetus, 54
equality principle, 36
equity principle, 36
escalation tactic, 120–121
expertise, as key to credibility, 46

facts
  importance of, 15
  lying about, 38
  and vivid information trap, 148–149

Index

fairness
  Aesop's fable on, 37
  and egos, 37
  need for clarity and simplicity, 37
  principles of, 36
fanaticism, 152
feedback, importance of, 7
Fields, W.C., 34, 152
first impressions, 50, 51
first offers
  aggressive, 80
  credible, 87
  forceful presentation of, 49
  guidelines for, 79
  high, 22, 80, 126
  importance of, 23, 78
  planning of, 22
  practicing defense of, 23
  reasonable, 80
  in relation-based negotiations, 81
  use of midpoint in, 9
  when BATNA is weak, 81
Fisher, Roger, 12
flexibility
  created by proposals, 70
  cultivating reputation for, 43
  need for, 88
Ford, Henry, 88
frames
  aligning, 147
  analyzing, 147
  defined, 146
Freud, Sigmund, 39
Freund, James C., 13
Frick, Henry Clay, 99
frustration, gestures indicative of, 178

Gates, Bill, 98
Gerber, J. Jay, 143
Gillespie, James J., 101
Gilovich, Thomas, 148, 156
Goldwyn, Samuel, 75, 122
good guy, bad guy tactic, 124–125
Goodman, Peter, 55

Haldeman, H.R., 28
Harris, Sydney J., 52

herd behavior, 156–157
Hindery, Leo Jr., 77, 95
Hopper, Grace Murray, 128
Hore-Belisha, Lord, 38
Horn, Sam, 4
Hubbard, Frank McKinney, 66
hubris, 136
Huizenga, Wayne, 127

IBM, 135
Ikle, F.C., 86
indifference, gestures indicative of, 177–178
innumeracy, 150
interests
  defined, 14
  emphasizing similarities in, 88, 89
  exploiting differences in, 86
  identification of, 15, 29
  as issues, 16
  long-term, 15
  lying about, 38
  reconciliation of, 14
issues
  avoiding single ones, 19
  avoiding weak ones, 19
  listing of, 18
  in logical chunks, 19
  ranking of, 16
  valuation of, 16, 17

Jordan, Henry, 36

Kahneman, Daniel, 138
Karass, Chester L., 19, 123, 131
Kautilya, 124
Kennedy, Gavin, 21, 25, 67
Kennedy, Joseph P., 14
Kiam, Victor, 50
Kiely, Laree S., 73
Kissinger, Henry A., 26
Koren, Leonard, 55
Kozol, Jonathan, 16

language, *see also* meta-talk
  assertive *vs.* aggressive, 56
  avoiding fillers, 57

language (*continued*)
  persuasive, 56–58, 59
  strong words, 57
  words that sell, 58
Lascheves, Sara, 83
lemming effect, 156–157
Lewicky, Roy J., 125
lie detection
  clues to deceit, 41
  nonverbal clues, 40
  training in, 40
Lincoln, Abraham, 11, 45
listening
  as aid to conflict resolution, 93
  persuasive, 54
  for signals, 66
  as telephone tactic, 162
Litterer, Joseph A., 125
Lorenzo, Frank, 129
loss
  avoidance of, 138
  tolerance for, 139
lying, *see* deceit

Mackay, Harvey, 6
Marx, Groucho, 110
Mayer, Robert, 63, 161, 163
McGovern, George, 20
mediators, 93
mergers
  deal frenzy, 159
  impact of overpaying, 158
meta-talk
  avoiding, 62–63
  defined, 62
  double meanings, 63
  examples of, 62
Metcalfe, David, 9
Microsoft, 135
Mills, Harry, 51
Mills One-Page Planner, 169
Minton, John W., 125
Mnookin, Robert H., 155
momentum, building of, 88–89
Morgan, J.P., 99, 119
multiple options, simultaneous offer of, 87

Murrow, Edward R., 46
myopia, 144–145

Napoleon Bonaparte, 109
need principle, 36
negative tactics, 110–111
negotiations, *see also* bargaining
  competition *vs.* cooperation, 5
  give-and-take nature of, 6
  interests *vs.* positions, 14
  loss of momentum, 88
  men's attitudes on, 82
  Mills' One-Page Planner, 169
  overcoming discomfort, 83
  performance assessment, 106, 107
  planning of, 168
  purpose of, 14
  relationship-based, 86
  retaining flexibility during, 21
  and self-interest, 6
  smart *vs.* dumb, 134
  strategic choices, 30
  successful, 69
  use of questions, 52
  walking away from, 7
  women's attitudes on, 82
negotiators
  changing, 93
  mistakes made by, 134–135
  reputation types, 42
  transaction-driven, 84
  win-lose, 154
Newton, Isaac, 134
nibbling tactics, 112–113
Norris, Floyd, 139
number blindness, 150–151

objectives, listing of, 17
observer, role of, 25
O'Connell, Fergus, risk management formula, 34–35
offers
  final, 118
  opening, *see* first offers
  "take it or leave it," 118
openness, gestures indicative of, 176

opponent
  analysis of, 28
  discovering position of, 49
  identifying interests of, 29
  observation of, 50
  recognizing bluff of, 28
outrageous demands
  dealing with, 127
  purpose of, 126
overconfidence, 136–137
  "discount," 137

Pacino, Al, 118
Packer, Kerry, 130
Paige, Satchel, 142
Peppert, Scott R., 155
Perot, Ross, 12, 24
persuasive language, 56–58, 59
persuasive listening
  acknowledging feelings, 55
  to create empathy, 54
  paraphrasing, 55
Plante, Jacques, 133
positions, *vs.* interests, 14
practice, importance of, 7
preferences, asking for, 87
price, need for certainty, 23
proposals
  checkpoints for, 181–182
  conditional, 71
  defined, 70
  flexibility created through, 70
  formula for rejecting, 73
  guidelines for, 73
  need for brevity, 71
  packaging of, 72
Puzo, Mario, 22, 76

questions
  to avoid, 53
  framing of, 147
  as key negotiation tools, 52

Raiffa, Howard, 9
Raleigh, Sir Walter, 113
reactive devaluation, 155
readiness, gestures indicative of, 178

Reagan, Ronald, 115
representations, *see* claims
reputation
  for flexibility, 43
  importance of, 42
  for toughness, 43
  types of, 42
reservation prices, 8
  lying about, 38
resources, exploiting differences in, 86
RESPECT
  seven step diagram, 1
  seven step formula, 4
reverse auction tactic, 130–131
reviewers, role of, 25
Reynolds, R.J., 79
Richardson, John, 9
risks
  avoidance of, 33
  management of, 34
  O'Connell formula, 34–35
  self-assessment, 32, 33
  "will-I-sleep-at-night" test, 33
Robertson, Corbin, 33
Rodman, Dennis, 101
Rogers, Will, 104
Ross, Steve, 154
Rosten, Leo, 70
Ruff, Howard, 144

Saki, 8
Santayana, George, 152
Sato, Ryoei, 158
Saunders, David M., 125
schmoozing, value of, 165
Schoonmaker, Alan N., 23
Schweitzer, Maurice, 38
Shehadie, Sir Nicholas, 114
Shell, G. Richard, 81, 165
short-term focus, 144–145
signalling
  checkpoints for, 181
  purpose of, 66
  reciprocating by, 67
  willingness to move, 67

Index

silence
  after initial offer, 79
  strategic use of, 60, 61
  as telephone tactic
single-issue focus, 155
Skopec, Eric Wm., 73
Spence, Gerry, 47
splitting the difference, 98–99
statistics
  unreliability of small numbers, 151
  and vivid information trap, 148–149
Stowers, James E., 151
strategy
  determining factors, 31
  four choices, 30
strength, revealing one's, 13
summary close, 96, 97
Sun-Tzu, 31, 96

tactics
  defined, 110
  negative, 110–111
  winning, 112–131
team
  allocation of functions, 25
  management of, 24
  selection of, 25
team leader, role of, 25
telephone
  effective use of silence, 60
  negotiating by, 162–163
tension, dealing with, 92
third party go-between, as negotiating option, 99
Thompson, Leigh, 7, 89
time management
  and deadline pressure, 26
  guarding against time trap, 27
  preparing a time plan, 26
  used to advantage, 31

toughness, cultivating reputation for, 43
Trump, Donald, 43, 84, 111
trust, as key to credibility, 46
Tulumello, Andrew S., 155
Turner, Ted, 136
Tversky, Amos, 138
Twain, Mark, 154

uncertainty, gestures indicative of, 178–179
Ury, William, 12, 97

Valery, Paul, 100
Vare, Daniele, 3
vivid information, 148–149

walking away
  knowing when, 153
  to reject terms, 7
  role-playing of, 159
  strategy, 119
Watkins, Michael, 5
weighing close, the, 98–99
Wendt, Gary, 36
West, Mae, 82
Whitehead, Alfred North, 146
Wilcox, Frederick, 32
Wilson, Earl, 106
win-lose mindset, 154–155
winner's curse, 158–159
Wolff, Bob, 57
women, as negotiators, 82
words
  emotive, 58
  persuasive, 59
  warm *vs.* cold, 58

Zone of Possible Agreement (ZOPA), 8

ABOUT THE AUTHOR

Harry Mills is the chief executive of The Mills Group, an international consulting and training firm, and has spent the last twenty years training many of the worlds top companies in the art and science of negotiation. The Mills Group's corporate clients include IBM, Ericsson, Oracle, BMW, Toyota, Lexus, and Unilever.

Harry Mills's professional service clients include the Big Four giants: PricewaterhouseCoopers, KPMG, Ernst & Young, and Deloitte. He is the best-selling author of twenty-three books on sales, persuasion and negotiation, including *The Rainmaker's Toolkit, Sales Secrets* and *The Mental Edge*. The American Chamber of Commerce called Harry's book, *Artful Persuasion: How to Command Attention, Change Minds and Influence People,* "one of the best books ever written on persuasion." He is also a subject-matter expert and mentor for the Harvard Business School Publishing's ManageMentor program on persuasion.

A regular keynote speaker at international conferences, Harry Mills appears regularly on television and radio to comment on business issues. He has been featured in *Entrepreneur* magazine, *BottomLine Business, Sales & Marketing Management* and *USA Today*. An accomplished dealmaker in his own right, Harry Mills has negotiated a number of billion-dollar-plus deals and has worked on complex negotiation topics such as mergers, acquisitions, and climate change.

Harry Mills can be contacted at *harry.mills@millsonline.com*. The Mills Group Web site, *www.millsonline.com,* offers further tools and a complete range of supporting services.